THE ARTS AND CITY PLANNING

AMERICAN COUNCIL FOR THE ARTS
570 Seventh Avenue, New York, NY 10018

Edited by Robert Porter

© Copyright 1980 American Council for the Arts

Additional copies may be obtained from:

ACA Publications
570 Seventh Avenue
New York, NY   10018

Library of Congress Cataloging in Publication Data

Main entry under title:

The arts and city planning.

    1. Artists and community--United States--
Addresses, essays, lectures. 2. Urban beautifi-
cation--United States--Addresses, essays, lectures.
3. Arts and society--United States--Addresses,
essays, lectures. I. American Council for the Arts.
NX180.A77A77   700'.1'03   80-14076
ISBN 0-915400-20-0

Cover Design: Greenboam & Casey Associates

Introduction

A stroll along the winding Riverwalk through the
heart of San Antonio, far below the hustle and
bustle on the street above, takes you past a
wealth of lush greenery, intimate restaurants
and cabarets, arts and crafts galleries, im-
promptu performances and festive people. The
beauty of the Riverwalk, its very human scale,
encourages a spirit of warmth in people which both
mirrors and magnifies the appeal of its ambiance.
It is, in short, a utopian marriage of culture--
of design, art, and performance--and astute city
planning.

It seems altogether fitting, then, that leading
city planners, arts administrators, and government officials from across the nation convened
in San Antonio in December 1979 to explore, for
the first time, the potential of such a marriage,
one between the arts and city planning. This diverse group came together sharing a mutual concern
for the vitality of our cities.

That such partnerships are possible, and potentially valuable, was perhaps best exemplified by
the breadth of the conference sponsors--the
American Council for the Arts, the American Planning Association, Partners for Livable Places, the
U.S. Conference of Mayors, the National League of
Cities, the Texas Commission on the Arts and the
Arts Council of San Antonio. And there could have
been no better friend or supporter of this conference than the Ewing Halsell Foundation and ACA
board member, Gilbert M. Denman, Jr., without
whose financial support the conference could not
have happened.

The following pages set forth the substance of the
conference, an assemblage of the perspectives and
perceptions of the nineteen major speakers at San
Antonio. Do not look for any simple solutions,
however, for there are none. The conference was
a time to explore ideas, to challenge them, to
understand each other, and to search for a common
ground. In truth, it was only the beginning, a
foundation upon which to build.

The great value of The Arts and City Planning Conference will only be realized if the concepts which
it helped to shape about integrated planning for
the arts--cultural planning--are brought to fruitior
An ad hoc group consisting of the American Council
for the Arts, the American Planning Association,
Partners for Livable Places, the U.S. Conference of
Mayors and the National League of Cities has been
formed to build upon the foundation created in San
Antonio. Its goal is to research, develop and implement strategies that will crystallize the concept of cultural planning, and to develop concrete
proposals for integrating the arts into comprehensive plans.

It will certainly not be an easy task, but the
enormous potential benefit to both the arts and to
our cities is reason enough to tackle the hard work
that lies ahead. We face, as Wolf Von Eckhardt so
aptly said in summing up the conference, "a promis-
ing beginning of finding new ways and mechanisms
for satisfying (the cultural craving) and for making both the arts part of city planning and city
planning part of the arts."

Annette Covatta
Director of Programs

Contents

The Arts and City Livability

by John L. Kriken
Director of Planning and Urban Design, Skidmore, Owings & Merrill

The arts share a common purpose with planning in helping to make a city livable. They also share a common situation; while interest for environmental quality grows, arts programs and planning programs are being challenged by budget limitations sweeping the country. This, then, would seem to be a timely moment to share the concerns of the arts and planning. The practice of planning deals broadly with all the land use subjects of the city: transportation, housing, commercial space, civic activities, open space, industry, etc. It is based on the assumption that public goals can be set and implemented through various governmental methods. It also assumes that the economic and political forces either favor change or retention of the status quo and can be guided or stimulated to some positive environmental purpose.

The practice of planning is most often based upon situations of either economic decline or rapid economic growth, both of which are often viewed as destructive to the quality of urban life and livability. For example, in San Francisco this could mean the introduction of tall buildings which disrupt the views and otherwise alter the fabric of the city's neighborhoods. In San Antonio, it may have meant the decline, or even removal, of historically interesting buildings for lack of an economic service role that they could play in the community. In both instances, the methods to treat these issues are different. In San Antonio, the problem was to discover incentives to stimulate economic activity. In San Francisco, on the other hand, the problem was to discover controls to guide growth to more positive patterns of development.

Both of these cities illustrate the linkage between culture and livability. And, perhaps more importantly, they illustrate the linkage between livability and the economic viability of the cities themselves.

Any discussion of San Antonio's urban character has to begin with its river. The San Antonio River is literally and figuratively the stage for the city's cultural, commercial and civic life. The city's first settlements, the most famous of which is the Alamo, were missions along the river's edge. A number of these missions have recently been designated as a national park and will thus be assured of preservation.

In the 1920s San Antonio was the financial center of Texas, and most of the city's older buildings date from that era. It was at this same time, however, that the river became a problem requiring flood control considerations. The community found itself with three choices. The first was simply to cover over the existing river bed and develop a flood bypass channel. The second was to abandon this below-street-level area to truck servicing. And the third, which is happily what happened-- thanks to a visionary mayor and citizenry--was to beautify the river, undertaken with the help of the Works Progress Administration (WPA).

San Antonio's river area is, in many people's opinion, one of the best pieces of urban design in America. It is literally a gallery, a place for art and a place for performance. Constantly maintained at thirty-feet wide, the river winds through the downtown area twenty feet below street level, offering a park-like contrast to the level above. Flood protection has enabled this area to have commercial activity along its banks. The river is the focus of most civic festivals, fiestas and parades which feature floats on the river.

In the 1940s San Antonio lost its position as a financial center both to Houston and Dallas and,

in fact, began a period of economic decline. In
the 1960s San Antonio's shaky economy was based
primarily on tourism and nearby military bases.
At this time the city leadership decided to attempt
to strengthen the economic base around tourism
through revitalization efforts in the downtown
area. From the onset the cultural facilities and
activities of the city were linked directly to the
strength of the city's economic base. A number of
projects were generated, notably the revitalization
of the downtown produce market which was a unique
cultural institution of the city.

Perhaps the most ambitious project was undertaken
on the east side of the city--to prepare San Antonio
as the site for the 1968 World's Fair, the HemisFair.
The idea was to use the fair as the economic stimu-
lus to create new cultural facilities to attract
tourism and to develop spin-off facilities such as
restaurants, hotels, and public relations services
to serve this segment of the economy. This new
project was closely connected, as it should have
been, to the river, and one can now visit these
facilities by river taxi or by walking along the
river walkways. The remaining facilities include
a 3,000-seat theatre for the performing arts, a
10,000-seat arena, the Tower of the Americas, and
the Texas Institute of Culture, an anthropological
museum dedicated to explore the different cultural
strains that have blended to produce Texas culture.

Other fair facilities have subsequently become part
of the University of Texas campus and the Mexican-
American Cultural Exchange Institute. A number of
hotels and restaurants continue to serve the city's
tourist trade.

In 1973 the city undertook to extend its livability
into downtown neighborhoods and again the idea was
to build off the river. But this time the idea was
to develop those unused parts of the river not
landscaped by the WPA and which were hidden behind

fences and parking lots. Unlike the vast urban renewal projects that characterized the 1960s, the plan was to locate rather small, but strategically important, investments that would start with flood control investments to finance engineering development, and then be coordinated with other supportive investments to unify, revitalize, and beautify the entire downtown area.

The objectives of the river flood control measures were essentially twofold. One objective was to conserve the river banks. In areas where this was not viable, consideration was given to widening the banks to create water features which coordinated with future neighborhood settings. This was then coordinated with a second objective, an extensive lineal park program, using the river as a pathway to various destinations along the river bank. A historic brewery building located on the river bank is now being converted to a major citywide art facility as well as part of a neighborhood center.

There are attendant problems which must be addressed to stimulate improved development along the river's banks. The consideration of transportation is essential both within the neighborhoods--for example, routing traffic to the edges of neighborhoods rather than through neighborhoods--and on a regional basis, including parking.

Additionally, housing programs were required to accommodate rehabilitation, spot in-fill, and the introduction of middle-income housing. In the King William area of San Antonio, for example, there are lovely, historic 100-year-old houses that have now been rehabilitated.

Physical improvements alone, however, do not guarantee livability. The city plans to develop a number of social services that are unique to the city in order to attract people from the suburbs. The strategy is based upon taking existing educational and cultural facilities and, by combining them, making a unique resource for the city.

In San Antonio one can clearly see all the strategies, all the city's energies, working to build and to extend the city's economy and, therefore, the city's livability.

In the city of San Francisco, circumstances are really quite the reverse. While in San Antonio the interest is in creating economic activity, in San Francisco it lies in slowing it down or guiding economic activity to less disruptive ends.

In the 1950s San Francisco was at best a regional center. The downtown area was made up mostly of ten- and twenty-story buildings. In the 1960s San Francisco became a desirable place not only for western states' corporate headquarters, but also for world headquarters of a number of companies and facilities. This created an incredible boom, a boom not only in absolute square footage, but also in the character of the city from a twenty-story scale to a scale that reaches sixty stories. By the 1970s citizens had begun to express concern about the relationship of these giant new buildings to the scale of existing buildings, which might now become overwhelmed. They feared the impact of this new development on the adjoining neighborhoods, such as the Telegraph Hill area, with respect to congestion and even spillover parking. And they expressed a growing concern about the cheap Disneyland-type environments designed to attract tourists which seemed to be springing up everywhere and threatening the quality of San Francisco.

In the early 1970s Allan Jacobs, then planning director for the city, completed the San Francisco urban design plan. This plan was an attempt to state very clearly some guidelines to control and protect more positively San Francisco's well-known

and admired physical character. Initially the
plan tried to identify what made San Francisco
unique, what makes it such a special place to
live. The effect of this was to give the citizens
of San Francisco some terms of reference, a vocab-
ulary to begin to speak of their concerns to the
decision makers and politicians of the city.

For example, as citizens expressed increasing
concern for some compatibility between new and
existing adjacent development, a law for controlling the height and bulk of new buildings was
instituted. The result was areas of tall buildings
that tapered down to the scale of existing districts
to be preserved, such as Chinatown and Jackson
Square.

The plan attempted to identify issues of quality,
function and livability. Once identified as city
policy they were used as standards to review and
judge future development proposals. The plan also
provided developers with the bonus of extra square
footage of building for providing certain amenities
believed to be in the public interest such as plazas.

A recent urban renewal project in San Francisco is
a good example of our shifting attitudes toward
development and city livability. The project is
called Yerba Buena Center. The intent of the
project, very much like the intent of San Antonio's
Hemisfair, was to develop convention facilities
which in turn could help revitalize a declining
area and channel new development away from historically sensitive areas such as Jackson Square.

Unfortunately the project, characteristic of early
1970s urban planning techniques, took the form of
a single huge piece of architecture where various
uses were layered, one on top of the other, sand-
wich style. Almost without exception, planners
now recognize this as bad urban design because it
is so extremely vulnerable to any kind of economic

breakdown. For example, if one of the layers
changes or experiences financial difficulty, then,
like a house of cards the entire concept crumbles.
Furthermore, such large projects are usually out of
scale with surrounding existing development.

A much more adaptable approach seems to be a return
to small parcel sizes and incremental development.
By returning to the sort of traditional building-
by-building development that historically has made
San Francisco and San Antonio great cities, we do
not fix use, but simply fix the standards of quality
which any system of uses would have to accommodate.
In this way we are not so vulnerable to the shifting
winds of the market place.

It is also possible to set up a sequence for what
is called market offerings, that is, determining
through a public process which uses are most desirable. Rather than simply putting a development
proposal together, putting it on the market and
having it collapse for lack of interest, we propose
to develop a sequence for these offerings, starting
with the most publicly desired, but not necessarily
the most feasible, and moving in a pre-established
sequence. Depending upon success in the marketplace, the final plan of land uses is selected.
Such an approach promises a diversity and richness
that grows out of many participants--developers,
architects and artists.

The open space of this project would be endowed
with a one percent amount for an art program. This
provides under state and city law that one percent
of the construction budget for publicly assisted
development projects is provided for the acquisition of sculpture or other appropriate art forms to
become part of the project's adornment. The visual
diversity of architecture and art is the best kind
of urbanism. It is why we find San Francisco and
San Antonio unique and exciting cities. But developing an urbanism that has the richness of historical

architecture and art in contemporary terms is a difficult task. It is not so much a question of taste as it is of cost. Our building forms are simple and often bland to the eye because craft skills have disappeared and, where they exist, are too expensive.

I have often imagined a development situation in which artists and art help to fill this gap. Through such a situation, WPA artists made the San Antonio River the unique place it is today by creating a diversity of landscape, bridges, paving, furniture, and lighting that could not be conceived by one individual.

Both San Antonio and San Francisco have based their revitalization and conservation programs on their culturally related livability. These are lessons many cities could profitably learn. There is also the lesson of the San Antonio River; its character reflects the participation of artists. This is an opportunity that needs to be rediscovered.

What Arts Organizations and Artists Can Offer City Planning

by Michael Newton
President, The Performing Arts Council of the Music Center of Los Angeles County

My concern with the place of the arts in the life of the city began thirteen years ago in St. Louis, a city for which I had, and have, continuing affection. As director of the Arts and Education Council, I believed that my task was to find ways to make the arts integral to the life of that city. Urban renewal had come to St. Louis in the late 1950s and early 1960s and its monument was the destruction of a goodly part of the historic housing stock of the city. By the time I came to the city, it resembled Dresden or Hamburg at the end of the Second World War. One problem was that the people who had lived in the overcrowded and rundown housing did not simply go away. They had to be re-housed at public expense. Re-housing took the form of a series of eleven high-rise buildings, each fourteen stories high, that at their peak were home to more than 75,000 persons. This complex bore the name Pruitt-Igoe and upon completion won national awards for the architects. In a very short period of time, however, Pruitt-Igoe had turned into the worst urban slum I have seen in four continents and in a lifetime of travel. Not until I saw the South Bronx had I ever seen so degrading a landscape of squalor, violence and hopelessness.

We at the Arts Council were invited by a despairing housing authority to devise some plan that could address the desolation and alleviate the suffering. Of course there wasn't any money, but there were spaces and there were people-- plenty of people. I would like to be able to say that we succeeded, that out of that experience

came great art and great performances. But
I doubt it. Eventually, in the 1970's, the
situation was so bad that Pruitt-Igoe was
destroyed, literally dynamited by the hands
that planned and built it.

While I was in St. Louis we built Powell
Symphony Hall, one of the most successful
examples of a recycled former vaudeville
house I have ever seen. Done with taste,
style and economy, it won plaudits throughout
the land. We were so proud of it that we
overlooked the fact that it stood isolated in
an area of rapid disintegration and decay.
Some thought it might anchor the area. What,
after all, could better hold the line of
retreat of the white middle class than the new
multi-million dollar home of the St. Louis
Symphony? But symphony-goers didn't really
do much for the neighborhood. They drove
there once, twice, three times a week, parked,
went to the concert, got back in their cars
and left. They didn't even stay for dinner.
The result was a fabulous hall which remained
an island. In retrospect, what is strange is
that we did not better involve the city in
safeguarding an investment. Nor did the city
have the sense to build on the asset that we
had created.

the 1960s were a time when outrage was
accompanied by determination that something
could be done. We felt outrage at what we and
our leadership were allowing to happen to a
once beautiful city and at how profligate we
had been with our heritage, our resources and
our hopes. Still, we believed that where there
was energy and will, there was a way. We
elected the director of the planning commission
to our board at the Arts Council and we engaged
in the planning process for the arts ourselves.
I was appointed chairman of the city's committee

for planning in the arts and juvenile delin-
quency. And that was progress.

In the 1970s, having learned something from
the preceding decades, we better understand
the virtues of continuity with the past
and of texture in our communities, and the
importance of neighborhoods. And we understand
that the arts have a role to play--in economic
as well as other terms. For example, we find
that artists can act as frontiersmen in opening
up abandoned or deprived areas of the city to
redevelopment. In exchange for inexpensive,
large spaces in which to live and work, artists
will put up with cold and dirt and hardships.
In their wake they bring a new middle class,
along with boutiques, condominiums, French
restaurants, exposed brick, outdoor sculpture
and all the other elements of the good life--
urban style. City government has been a partner
in this change by granting the zoning variances
on which the change is based. The only problem
is that once gentrification has set in, the
artists typically can no longer afford to live
in the neighborhood. Few cities have developed
protection for the pioneers.

Another example of the relationship of the arts
to city development is in the creation of major
performing arts centers that provide anchors
for once decaying downtowns or for the neighborhoods in which they are built. Developers with
office buildings, banks, hotels and parking
facilities move in behind the performing arts.
Land values rise, employment spreads and adver-
tisements appear in national magazines heralding
the new Atlanta, Los Angeles, Milwaukee, etc.
Ironically, the performing arts often do not
share in the increase of wealth that they have
generated--so there is a phenomenon such as
Lincoln Center that legitimately claims responsibility for the revival of the west side of

Manhattan but within which the Beaumont Theatre
has been dark for two years for lack of funding.
Then, too--as in the case of Powell Symphony Hall--
the people who attend some of these centers often
do not come to the area for much more than the
performances. Too many centers only come to life
four hours a day.

If other developments prosper when the arts take a
lead, so, too, can a commercial development like
a shopping center be made more successful with
the engagement of the arts. Artists displaying
or demonstrating their wares, a performing group
presenting a short piece, classes in dance or
pottery or painting can all help to elevate the
shopping experience to something of quality beyond
the ordinary. The arts festival can celebrate
civic pride in and enjoyment of downtown or of a
neighborhood by attracting tens of thousands of
persons to events where art is demonstrated and
sold, performed and applauded and where exotic
foods are cooked, smelled, sold and consumed.

Memorials more lasting than weekend arts festivals are the commissioned works of art and sculpture that adorn and brighten some of our public
buildings. Many of these works, however, are
set in deserted public spaces to be viewed
suspiciously from a distance by upright citizens
and up close only by the winos and bums who are
the principal habitues of many of these spaces.

Nevertheless, these instances of the incorpora-
tion of the arts are changes for the better.
I suspect they have not come about principally
because of either the arts or the planners but
rather because the arts in our society have
entered the mainstream of middle-class life and
experience. ACA has provided a great public
service by commissioning and publishing the Lou
Harris "Americans and the Arts" studies. These
studies demonstrated to a suspicious and unbe-

lieving art world how the audience for the arts
and the number of participants in the arts had
grown. No longer are the arts the province of
a band of pilgrims distinguished by the paucity
of their numbers and the purity of their thought.
Suddenly we recognized what the lines at our
museums, the demand for tickets at our theatres,
the explosion of dance, the sales of classical
records and musical instruments have been telling
us: that a new generation of better educated,
more affluent Americans has different expectations of life--and among those expectations is
participation in the arts.

Our leadership, as Lou Harris has pointed out,
lagged behind the public in its awareness of this
change. Many of the problems of the arts and of
their limited impact on our neighborhoods, towns
and cities have arisen from the tendency to place
them not at the center but at the periphery of
our social ordering. This was not always so.
In the early days of the republic, the arts and
everyday pursuits were comfortably lodged together,
often, indeed, in the same person. But in this
century it has been different. What a curious
concept, for example, lies behind that estimable
program of percent-for-art in architecture--as if
art and architecture are separable, as if art is
something you stick on after the building is built.

We see the same myopia in the displacement of
the artist from new areas of settlement. When
the pioneering is done, it is found the artist
needs too much space and is a trifle dirty for
the sanitized new environment. Anyway, we have
the art gallery, who needs the artist? We must
find ways to safeguard the housing/working space
of artists through zoning variances and through
a degree of subsidy. Half-entrepreneurs, half-
workers, they are like few others in our society,
and because of their contributions they must be
provided for. Such programs will mean inter-

vention in the free play of the market--but
we do that for the elderly, for farmers, for
schools and churches, for Chrysler. Why not
for those who extend our urban frontiers?

Artists, performers and representatives of
the arts community should be included in the
planning process. They belong on the city or
county planning commission, on staff and as
consultants. One of the functions of such
representatives should be to raise questions
about the effect of planning decisions on the
lives of citizens. This implies answers to cultural impact questions, similar to questions about
ecological impact. Virtually every decision
made by local government, whether it is in
signage,, in public transportation or building
of schools, parks or libraries, involves
aesthetic judgments. These judgments may be
made by default, but they are made nonetheless.
There should be someone in the decision-making
process to speak on behalf of the harmonious,
the pleasing and, yes, the beautiful. When
Boris Goldmund first dealt with the public
transportation company in Cincinnati, he
found the company proposed to set up a new set
of bus shelters in that city in the dead of
night because it feared the proposed shelters
were so unattractive that there would be a
public outcry. People *do* care what their cities
look like. In the 1960s in St. Louis, school
children broke windows in their schools and
the response was the building of schools without windows. The schools had slits like
medieval castles. And when a prison environment is created, people behave as if they were
in prison.

It is easier than it used to be for planners
to deal with the arts community and to secure
their involvement because the arts community
is more organized than it used to be and more

accustomed to working together. Every state
now has a public agency (with staff) that is
designed to serve the arts. Many of these
agencies are themselves engaged in the planning
process. Many are ably led. They should be
able to identify the key arts movers in individual communities. Similarly, many communities
now have local arts agencies, commonly called
arts councils or commissions. They run the
gamut from being first-rate to being unrepre-
sentative and ineffective, from being powerhouses to having few assets other than mimeo
machines and out-of-date mailing lists. Some
are private, some are public, but that is no
clue to how effective they are. The best arts
agencies are representative of artists, of the
public for the arts, of small organizations and
of major arts organizations. These agencies can
be especially useful for information on how to
involve artists in the planning process. This
is a difficult task since you first have to
identify the needs of the artists and performers
themselves. Once you bring the artists together,
you are in for a tough time--with one thousand
discordant voices resulting in the survival of
the noisiest while the best will probably be
driven away. A local arts agency can be used
for this function if it is a good one.

Different arts organizations can be useful in
different ways. You need to know their capabilities and their strengths. A major institution such as a symphony orchestra can give lustre
and stature to an important area but is too large
and inflexible for a host of localized uses. It
is more logical to match neighborhood needs with
neighborhood assets. Given the increase in
demand for the arts, wherever we provide for
neighborhood sports or recreational purposes,
we should provide for neighborhood cultural uses.
What is always universally true is that quality
counts. Having a third-rate theatre or a festi-

val without quality control will not benefit the community over the long haul.

It is said that the performing arts center is a concept whose time is done. There is talk of edifice complexes and elitism. (An "elitist" in arts parlance is anyone who raises more money than you do.) I would not argue for the arts center on theological grounds--that it is good per se. The strength of such centers is that they create critical mass which means not just a concentration of performances but of funding. Money in the arts, as in so much else, begets money. The criticisms of performing arts centers have arisen, I believe, because of two short-comings. First, many centers are architecturally uninspired--looking as if they had been ordered by Mussolini over the telephone. Secondly, they commonly lack a concern for pedestrian activity and movement.

There is, however, an opportunity to marry arts centers with housing, shops, or government offices. The Musuem of Modern Art Tower in New York is a good idea not just because of the revenue it will generate, but because it will involve people. The function of planners can be to bring the arts leaders together with developers or others who wish to build in a way that is compatible with arts needs. The arts leaders themselves may not think of that kind of marriage, but a planner can help by suggesting that the large numbers of persons who attend arts events are also represen-tative of middle class interests. Not that they want to surrender specialness or even opulence. The audiences appreciate comfort and some grandeur and mystery but they also like to be close to other people, to shop, and to be able to eat and drink. They attend the arts--as the Harris studies show--for a social as well as a cultural experience. "Let them communicate their enthu-siasm with their elbows," said Tyrone Guthrie.

So much of the structure of our society isolates
us as human beings: Our cars are isolation
booths; our suburban housing reflects a search
for seclusion; our urban high-rise apartments
stress security and anonymity; public spaces
often preclude sitting--as if the act of sitting
were an idle retreat from the public duty of
shopping.

In contrast, the arts are a social experience.
There is a good reason why the long-playing
record did not kill off attendance at symphony
concerts, why films did not replace theatre and
why the rise of television has coincided with
the greatest increase in audience for the performing and visual arts in our history. What
the arts can do is release us from a state of
being alone and remind us of our dependence on
others and their dependence on us. The arts
remind us of the paradox of our species: that
man can only fulfill his private passions, ideas
and dreams by sharing them with others.

Planning for the Arts

by Michael J. Pittas
Director, Design Arts Program, National
Endowment for the Arts

Coming from the Design Arts Program of the
National Endowment for the Arts to San Antonio
for a conference on cultural planning is like
returning to Delphi to consult the oracle, and
to have a *second* chat on the future of our
cities. For the city of San Antonio has had
some renowned seers. The first President of
the San Antonio Conservation Society, founded in
1924, was an artist, Emily Edwards, who saw how
a flood control project could lead to the development of today's handsome waterways. And San
Antonio's own O'Neil Ford, the godfather of the
Paseo Del Rio, is a former member of the National
Council on the Arts, and a founder of the Design
Arts Program within the Arts Endowment. Recently
the Design Arts Program has been able to be of
some help in the realization of the visions of
Ms. Edwards and Mr. Ford: Through an Endowment
grant and help from Johns Hopkins University,
a plan for a San Antonio performing arts district
has been created.

The fact that the arts constitute a major
industry in San Antonio, employing over 5,000
people and generating more than $50 million
annually, was a persuasive economic argument for
creating the district. In implementing the plan,
the principal concern has been for housing the
arts--that is, finding permanent homes for the
more than 1,000 performances a year which occur
in the city. The success of this plan is a
lesson in the benefit of cooperation between
public and private sectors, in the value of small
scale, incremental work and of careful attention
to the physical as well as the cultural and

historical fabric. San Antonio can serve as a symbol of the viability of both the Design Arts Program and cultural planning itself.

If cultural planning is becoming a concept with potential for broad application, it is probably because cities are in a second and very important state of transition. Post-World War Two American cities lost their middle-class populations as people migrated to the suburbs in quest of affordable single-family housing, better schools and safe streets. And sometimes their jobs followed as employers sought space for expansion and retailers exploited the captive market. Lately, however, there are signs that the urban exodus may be waning or even reversing.

Cities may no longer care to attract space-consuming, air-polluting industry to their cores. But cities are always the centers of banking, insurance, advertising, publishing, law, medicine, education, culture, entertainment and tourism. Today's newcomer to the city tends to be young, educated and middle-class, and wants to work in a white-collar occupation by day and enjoy the cultural and entertainment resources of the city by night. But the skyrocketing cost of high-rise apartment housing has spurred interest in the renovation and restoration of older buildings and has led to the revitalization of older neighborhoods. Residents are organizing to once again assume an active role in preserving and improving their communities.

The value of the planning profession in these changing times is re-emerging. And the new term, "cultural planning," helps to focus attention on the opportunity to integrate the arts into the everyday experience of urban residents. Since access to the arts is often what raises a community from bearable to livable, cultural planning should assure such access. Work has begun in this area. An article by Jerry Hagstrom about Winston-Salem, North Carolina, in the *National Journal* reads:

"An abandoned 1920s movie palace will be turned into a new performing arts center, attracting tourists and conventioneers from several states. A former Cadillac showroom will become an arts and crafts school complete with lighted, indoor parking to attract suburbanities. A vacant lot will be landscaped into a park and concert plaza where office workers may enjoy a leisurely lunch at a sidewalk cafe or watch a strolling minstrel or mime. Visitors may shop in a community art gallery in the old YMCA, or attend a traveling Smithsonian exhibition in an old hosiery mill.

Such is the future of downtown Winston-Salem, according to the visions of cultural, political and business leaders in the city of 140,000 persons. After twenty years of revitalization efforts that netted only a pedestrian mall so inactive that even the pawn shop has closed, the local leadership has decided that the arts will bring people back downtown. The arts, they say, offer people something they can't get from a suburban shopping center."

Mayor Maynard Jackson of Atlanta in the same publication saw the arts in a broader role-- as contributors to civic pride. He said, "The arts reveal us to ourselves. They show us who we are and where we are going, whether as a neighborhood, a city or a nation. The arts are an expression of community identity in its highest form."

Awareness of the value of cultural planning is becoming apparent in a variety of areas. Harvard and Berkeley, just to name two schools, have graduated a number of students in the last five years whose master's theses were on cultural planning. Harvey Perloff's study of Los Angeles began with discussions with the Arts Endowment in 1977. The United States Conference of Mayors produced an excellent publication which makes a strong case for the economic sense of planning

for culture in the city, and the National League
of Cities, with the American Council for the
Arts, sponsored a workshop on this general sub-
ject in December 1977 in San Francisco. Partners
for Livable Places, since its development in 1977,
has had cultural planning as one of its main goals.

The National Endowment for the Arts and its Design
Arts Program has a role to play in this process.
Grant applications to the Design Arts Program
provide a window, a national perspective, on
problems to be addressed by cultural planners.
One such problem is the location of new cultural
facilities. Easily acquirable tracts of land on
the outskirts of cities may appear attractive at
first. Wolf Trap, in the Virginia suburbs of
Washington, D.C., was successful until gas short-
ages caused its audiences to dwindle. When Dallas
passed a bond program for a new arts museum and
a new symphony hall, however, foresighted people
sought and received a small Design Arts Program
grant to perform extensive locational analysis
studies. They selected a center-city site.
Seattle is in the midst of controversy over the
location of its new opera house and art center
and has not, so far, moved toward a planning-
oriented solution.

Another problem is the displacement of artists
and their activities after their presence has
made an area fashionable for business and residential use. A Design Arts Program grant helped
the Arts Council of Minneapolis consider the
possible displacement impact of such "success" in
connection with a rezoning scheme converting a
warehouse area into an arts district.

Economic imperatives have been used to justify
greater public attention on cultural needs in
the cities of Winston-Salem and San Antonio.
In both instances, the principal art forms given
attention were the performing arts. And in both

cases the principal physical impact on the built environment came in the form of proposals to preserve and adapt older structures, many of which are of great historic and architectural significance

Attention to the built environment--the places and spaces in which cultural activities occur-- is a measure of our cultural heritage. Our architecture, the urban landscape, our civic spaces are at once that which shelters and houses our art forms and are also our most pervasive and enduring cultural legacy. Thus, when some of our architects propose great faceless, spanking new, travertine and marble monuments to the arts-- affronts to the very idea of urbanity--we should not unwittingly be seduced. We should help the design and planning professionals "use what is reusable" and relate what must be built anew to that which has come before.

Up until this point, I have referred to the fine arts--the performing and visual arts--as the manifestation and illustration of our cultural wealth from which planners can draw inspiration. Let me add that this country, above all nations, has contributed to the definition of culture the notion of "popular culture." Popular culture, for all its "low brow" connotations--the rock concert, the county fair, the Las Vegas spectacular, the ethnic street festival--is as important to the idea of cultural planning as those forms we normally associate with the "high brow" and the "elite." In many ways these populist urges, appealing to specific groups, to the young, the ethnic neighborhoods, the agricultural communities, or other interest groups and subcultures, reinforce the richness and diversity of America. To ignore these forces in the planning for the arts in urban areas would be to inappropriately "sanitize" the whole idea of cultural planning. Thus, when planners speak of "cultural planning," they should not only propose the recreation of the Kennedy and Lincoln Center ideas, but should also be speaking of creating the time, space, and places for more prosaic forms of cultural expression.

Above all, cultural planners should reach out to find what is unique in the diversity of our people and their "local" cultural aspirations, and, in doing so, help to bring into being theatre districts, galleries, museums, civic spaces, and places of public gatherings which are specific to those communities.

The Endowment, in trying to focus attention upon these issues, has, through its many programs, developed specific grant categories to assist communities with their cultural needs. I have redirected the Design Arts Program's 1980/81 Guidelines for our funding categories to focus upon the following: cultural *district* planning; design and planning of links between cultural facilities and other community activities such as transportation, shopping, working, and housing; housing the arts: providing artists with space for performance, exhibition, teaching, living, and working; design of special objects needed to execute a particular art form such as a safe, collapsible floor for use by dance touring companies; planning to ensure that artists, often the pioneers of community revival are not dis-placed as land values increase; design for the adaptive reuse of old buildings as new cultural facilities.

We are not a movement without roots. Diverse interests have taken individual steps in the direction of cultural planning. But the field will be defined by many more such "starts" around the country. Meanwhile, cooperation, not "turfdom," must be the rule of the day. Through diversity we will achieve the goal of common benefit.

An Orientation to Arts Agencies

I. by Elizabeth Howard
President, National Assembly of Community Arts Agencies

What is this thing called a local arts agency? When we opened our office in New York State, the state arts council called almost immediately to say: "Now that you are open, tell us what a local arts agency is." Nobody could quite come to terms with a definition.

One reason why it is difficult to come up with a single definition of a local arts agency is the very nature of its existence. Local arts agencies are the result of what is happening in particular geographic areas. Since no two geographic areas are alike, the arts agencies may function in different ways.

Basically, however, a local arts agency is a nonprofit, public or private agency that functions primarily as a support system and a network to develop, sustain and deliver quality arts in the community.

These functions may be carried out in a number of ways. Some arts agencies are primarily involved with providing services to artists, arts organizations and the general community. They may work cooperatively with various institutions in that area. Other arts agencies are primarily involved with presenting different kinds of arts programs and services, particularly in areas that might be described as culturally deprived. They all may be involved in such activities as audience development, fundraising, promotion of individual artists, development of an arts facility or the overall planning and development of the cultural life of a community.

We have heard that artists, performers, and
representatives of arts organizations are
involved in the cultural planning process.
We are looking for that kind of linkage from
the local arts agency in helping to build a
strong and culturally vital community.

II. by Robert Canon
Executive Director,
Arts Council of San Antonio

The Arts Council of San Antonio originally
was not very different from the majority of
arts agencies in the country. Started in 1964,
it was a nonprofit, private association of
individual arts organizations. The impetus
for the council was the perceived need to
"coordinate" the arts at a local level. The
arts agency was to serve as a clearinghouse
to report to the community on the activities
of the arts as well as to provide certain kinds
of services to arts organizations.

The notion that the Arts Council of San Antonio
should be an aggressive, developmental agency
for all the arts of the community, having
strong links to government and the private
sector, was theoretically implicit in its char-
ter, but this concept was never really put into
practice by the founders. There was no broad-
based community support for an arts agency,
and what support existed came from those who
believed the purpose of an arts agency was
to serve the interests of a select group of
arts institutions.

Then, in 1975, the agency was reorganized
under professional direction as a mechanism
to deal with the highly complex cultural
problems of a major urban area. The council
then had a budget of only $10,000 a year,
almost exclusively from membership dues.

Fortunately, in 1976, we received a grant
from the National Endowment for the Arts,
through a visionary program that no longer
exists, called City Spirit, which for the
first time made money available to cities to
plan for the arts. The arts council was also
able to get matching funds from the city for
the first time to begin the real development
of our agency.

These monies came at a very opportune time
for us because the city had just completed a
community development project in which it had
identified some eighteen individual districts
as priority targets for redevelopment. Acknowledging that the arts development needs of a city
historically correlate with overall urban
development needs, we were able to tap into
the districting effort already completed by
the city, in some cases consolidating these
districts for our purposes. Then we went
into each district to identify and catalogue
the cultural resources that existed, what
sorts of arts institutions were available and
what kinds of people--artists, key volunteers
of arts organizations, teachers, etc.--lived
in each district. As predicted, districts
that were essentially devoid of arts institutions, arts programs or people in the arts
were those same priority areas targeted for
development by the city.

The Arts Council of San Antonio accordingly
shaped its development around broad-based
community concerns. We were the first arts
agency in the country actually to establish
its own planning office. We also hired an
urban planner whose responsibility was to work
with the city's planning office to coordinate
their information with ours, to merge arts
needs with overall community needs to assure
an effective, comprehensive urban plan.

A great deal of our work was concerned with
research and planning. But trying to explain
to arts institutions, or even to artists, why
such a process is necessary can become very
controversial. The arts are not known for
planning. It is a new concept, to say the least,
and even the largest of our arts institutions
rarely know where they are going to be in two
years, much less five years.

To aid in our research and planning, we conducted a series of community meetings throughout the city. From the feedback at these
meetings, we determined there was a general
desire for regional professional arts centers,
similar to the branch library system, to be
established in various areas of the city.
Residents from all areas of the city expressed
a wish for access to some sort of center
where they could go to enjoy performances
and exhibitions and to participate in the
arts. This understanding led us to a plan
which, over a period of time, will establish
in the city a series of regional professional
arts centers, the first of which is already
in operation.

We have tried to work with as many arts organizations as possible (the number of arts
organizations in San Antonio has more than
doubled in the last three years) to develop
the beginning of a plan for the arts and the
establishment of the regional arts centers.
We determined that the city had established
several important arts facilities. There
was already one major art museum and another
underway, the new San Antonio Museum of Art
to be housed in an old brewery. The old
Ursuline Convent had been turned into a crafts
center. But when we began to think about the
performing arts, we realized there was no

central facility. Six theatres in the downtown area were either closed or only partly
operational. So the council organized a
committee to launch a study of those six theatres.

The Majestic Theatre, built in 1929, is one
of the last great movie palaces in America.
Its interior has been proposed as a concert
hall and home for the San Antonio Symphony.
The Symphony currently performs in a space
called The Theatre for the Performing Arts,
which is a part of the convention center complex. The problem here is that the convention
business has become more and more lucrative
in San Antonio, and the competition for the
space has become greater. A permanent residence for the Symphony would be far preferable.
A smaller theatre, the Empire, will become
a place to accommodate smaller events, such
as chamber dance performances and theatre.

An office building is stacked on top of the
Empire Theatre and another is in front of the
Majestic. Our idea is to create a complex
which would be essentially supported by
revenues from the parking garage and retail
and commercial leasing. Subsidized space in
these buildings could then be used by arts
organizations and by individual artists as
studios, rehearsal rooms, etc.

It is interesting to note that the most pes-
simistic group we have had to deal with has
not been the city officials, the politicians
nor the business and corporate communities.
It has been the arts organizations. We have
tried to quell some understandable fears by
assuring arts people that major consideration
has been given to ensuring that the arts
won't ultimately be pushed out of the complex
and that the complex will not become so expensive as to be finally prohibitive to the users.

What is occurring in San Antonio is really
not remarkable. It can happen and is happening in many cities in the country. There
is a network in almost every city of significant, professionally run arts agencies that
generally have a very clear idea about what
is happening in the arts in that city, where
the arts are going or where the arts should
go. They recognize that a linkage between
planning office, planning agencies and community arts agencies is essential. Most
arts agencies today want to tie in effectively
to the overall planning process of a city
to help enhance urban livability and cultural
vitality.

III. by Milton Rhodes
Executive Director, The Arts Council, Inc.

The Arts Council, Inc., in Winston-Salem,
North Carolina, is now almost thirty-one years
old. There has been quite a history of private
sector volunteer involvement in all phases of
growth. Now the public sector, during the
past five or six years, has become more
heavily involved in development in Winston-
Salem, particularly arts development.

In the past five or six years The Arts Council,
Inc., has served as a catalytic third sector
to unite government and business--on common
ground. The Arts Council as a whole is com-
posed of individuals with different points
of view who can come together and discuss
things openly, positively and as substantively
as possible. We have brought together people
who had not talked to each other in quite
some time, if at all--different racial mixtures,
different age mixtures, different socio-
economic groups, etc.

One of the strengths of the program in Winston-Salem has been the continued success of the united campaign for the arts, which offers a broad-based funding support network for local cultural institutions and arts agencies. It was started in 1958 after the building of one of the first combined arts centers, containing a 420-seat community theatre, a 7-room facility for the teaching of arts and crafts, and offices for the arts council, the children's theatre, the Civic Ballet and various other arts organizations. The Chamber of Commerce and the United Way, along with community leadership, primarily business leadership, raised the money for the center. They housed the Arts Council in a facility that provided access to their business resources to help in planning and development as well as the skills to contact the various other resources available to us throughout the community.

The year 1958 was probably one of the most significant times in our council's history, because finally the arts were allowed into the corporate board rooms for perhaps the first time with a united approach for giving to the arts. Our united campaign now raises more than $450,000 from 10 percent of the families in our community--more than 7,000 contributors.

In 1971 the Arts Council, Inc., underwent a change in its operating philosophy. The results of a long-range planning study convinced us we were not in the business of serving *only* the arts institutions in our community. We were in the business of serving the whole community on behalf of the arts. Therefore, we changed from a representative board of directors where each member group selected a representative, to a community-at-large board. In other words, instead of having the representatives from the symphony, community theatre, film organizations, etc., guiding or directing the organization, we chose people to run the arts council from the community at large.

In 1974 we undertook an attitudinal study, with Louis Harris and the National Research Center for the Arts, and their findings advised us to get out into the neighborhoods. Despite our then twenty-five-year involvement in the community, most people had never heard of us. We began a program of going into the neighborhoods with a series of mini-festivals provided by a grant from the National Endowment for the Arts. Thirty-one neighborhood festivals were organized and culminated in major street festival downtown which was financed by Schlitz.

In 1978 the council moved into downtown Winston-Salem, and since that time a number of private developers have started construction around the two-block area currently under the plan. This is all very stimulating to the state of the arts and to the revitalization of our center city.

A general philosophy has guided Winston-Salem through most of the years fairly successfully; Large numbers of volunteers from business, government and foundations deeply involved in all phases of the program's decision making are the key to a continued thriving cultural life for our cities. The Arts Council, Inc. is proud of the part it has played in encouraging such involvement during its thirty-year history.

An Orientation to the Planning Process

I. by Alan L. Canter
Director of Planning,
City and County of Denver

Planning can be defined as the basis for intelligent government action. Another definition of planning is a process within the framework of government. Another is a process of government which looks to the future for the purpose of influencing the well-being of the people. Finally, planning is essentially a process of understanding human needs and then influencing and shaping future public policy in order to serve those needs most effectively. The key word is process. Process is really what planning is all about.

It is not, however, the function of planning to assert general jurisdiction over operating departments. For example, it is not the planner's function to rule on the placement of street lights, traffic signals or policemen to control traffic. But it is within the province of the planning process to consider the width of streets, the use of one-way street systems and the location of major thoroughfares, because all of these factors are important to overall economic and social conditions. We have no reason to be concerned with the actual construction of sewer or water lines, but we are interested in the placement of them because where they go is economically, socially and demographically significant. Thus, while we do not construct and seldom implement, we are an integral part of the actual policy-making process essential to the delivery of an urban system.

There are four general areas with which planners are concerned. The first is quantitative planning. Planning has become increasingly quantitative because of the complexities brought about by the expansion of the basic responsibilities of the field. From a preoccupation with physical design and city scale, we have moved to a concern for the interrelatedness of social, economic and physical analyses and programming at all levels of government. Over the next several years, planning may be expected to make greater use of quantitative techniques, in both the demand for more and better data as a means of support for other interests, and in the continuing advances in the basic mechanics and procedures themselves.

The second area of concern is aesthetic planning. Design is a versatile, wonderful word as well as an uncomfortable one for the planning business. It is generally taken by the public to mean either the overall appearance of the community or the arrangement of separate buildings and projects. Neither stereotype is fully workable in the professional sense. Design in urban planning is directed at the distribution of a whole settlement of buildings, activities and open spaces, rather than at single objects or systems of public facilities.

Current achievements in design have been confined largely to such utilitarian areas as suburban shopping areas, college campuses and downtown office blocks. This is the dilemma faced by the contemporary planner. On the other hand, it is widely felt, both within the profession and among members of the public, that overzealous restrictions place too great a constraint on the developer. However, it is also true that the public asks the planner increasingly for a higher standard of environment.

Under these circumstances planners have tried a number of approaches: (i) Design by government

of an entire city, such as Brasilia or Chandigarh;
(ii) Control of the key facilities of a city,
such as the boulevards laid out by Georges
Haussmann in Paris; (iii) Design of publicly
owned property, public buildings, parks and
highways; (iv) Rebuilding of deteriorating
areas through such measures as urban renewal,
beautification and acquisition of open spaces.
These approaches are particularly significant
because they accomplish two objectives that
have been the cornerstone of our political sys-
tem--the avoidance of perpetual ownership of
land by government and the fusion of the efforts
of government with private enterprise.

The third general area of concern to planners
is the political arena. It was not so long ago
that planners considered themselves aloof from
politics. No experienced professional maintains
such a view today. The planner is now interested
in seeing his or her proposals implemented, and
he or she participates in various ways in the
process of implementation. In some cases, the
planner is directly attached to the office of
the chief executive and consequently in the fore-
front of political stress. The result is that
the planner has become aware of a number of
phenomena, however shadowy and elusive, that
can hinder the success of his or her program.
One such phenomenon is the power structure of
the community--that collection of movers and
shakers, public and private professionals,
who provide a touchstone for public proposals.

Citizen participation is also a part of the
political process. The federal government is
especially concerned with the consensus aspect
of planning, and it has consistently made its
constituents part of the planning program of
the community, including each renewal project
that it undertakes.

These are factors external to the technical
program but important nevertheless. Internally,
the planner is concerned with perfecting the
tools of management--with being able, on one
hand, to keep the broad perspective with which
he or she is charged, and yet, at the same time,
to fulfill individual assignments in relation
to one another and to the larger picture.

Planners know, too, that they must work closely
with the legislative body and the chief admin-
istrator, not only on the physical developments
of planning, but also on budgeting, programming,
intergovernmental negotiations and socio-economic
research, to see that plans are put into effect.

The fourth and final area of concern to planners
is social planning and social welfare. The
city planning that has been practiced in this
country has demonstrated tacit acceptance of
the doctrine that the physical environment is
a major determinant of social behavior and
individual welfare. As the complex web of inter-
relationships in our society is revealed, however, the simplistic concentration on the physical has given way. For example, we find that
in renewal schemes equal emphasis must now be
given to highly personalized elements--relocation
as well as reconstruction, social adjustment
to a new environment as well as adjustment of
utilities.

In large measure these changes can be traced to
a shift in focus in the nation as well as in
the profession itself. As a people we have discovered and recognized that amid affluence there
exist pockets of severe poverty. Elimination
of this poverty has taken on the status of a
national purpose. It is likewise acknowledged
that hand in hand with economic inequality go
other ills: discrimination, lack of education
and physical deterioration.

Within city planning, the urgencies presented
by these ills, as well as the opportunities
afforded to alleviate them, have turned the
spotlight away from the urban fringe areas
and smack dab upon the inner cities. Thus,
planning finds itself enmeshed in problems of
race, income and social disorganization. When
the courts speak, they declare that the schools
must be planned as foci of social interaction.
They say that zoning cannot classify land so
that low-income groups are, in effect, excluded
from the community.

The area of urban social welfare is still largely
uncharted, both for planners and for social
welfare workers whose responses are geared to
individual clients rather than to the broad
spectrum of the municipality.

The nature of our system today means that a
planning department is involved in a multitude
of areas. The Denver Planning Office, for
example, is involved in law enforcement, police,
administration, fire prevention and protection,
safety programs, public health protection,
public welfare, capital improvement, control
and abatement of nuisances and water, air and
noise pollution, energy conservation, education
and culture, historic preservation and a multitude of other nontraditional planning programs.
We have changed our emphasis as planners from
in-state comprehensive planning for a specific
point in time to a policy plan approach.

We are now creating policies that are flexible
in order to facilitate technological and economic
changes. These policies encompass the gamut of
concerns of city development, and they provide
the elected leadership with effective guideposts
for the successful development of the city.

II. by Allan B. Jacobs
Chairman, Department of City and Regional Planning, University of California at Berkeley

I've been asked to comment briefly, all too briefly, on a number of questions, namely: Who are city planners? What do they do? How might what they do relate to the arts?

Who are city planners? They are mostly people with graduate degrees in city and regional planning. Some have undergraduate degrees in urban studies. And some, especially in larger cities, have no formal training in city planning. They come to their jobs via such routes as the civil service examination. City planners have undergraduate backgrounds in just about every discipline imaginable. Architecture used to be the most common background for city planners, but not any more. Increasingly, economics, sociology, political science, landscape architecture, law, engineering and the humanities--history, languages, journalism--are providing the academic backgrounds for planners.

In graduate schools future planners specialize in sub-fields such as land use planning, urban design, housing, community development (which includes citizen participation techniques), transportation planning, regional planning and development and planning for public services. Most graduate programs in the field require two years of study.

City planning is well established at the local level of government. This is important because it suggests something about what city planning departments can and cannot do and how they view things. Most city planning staffs operate under city planning commissions. That is, the professional staff reports to a group of seven to eleven lay commissioners appointed by a mayor. The idea was, and still may be, to remove the commission and the staff from daily

Generally speaking, the arts are not the highest priority area with which city planning
offices have had to deal. On the other hand,
it is interesting that when San Francisco did
an urban design plan in the late 1960s and
early 1970s, they had poets, sculptors and
other artists as part of their advisory team.

City planning departments are involved, usually
by law, with capital improvement programming.
The standard function of capital improvement
programming is basically to decide where to
spend dollars for public capital improvements.
Most planning departments are, in one way or
another, involved in that sort of activity.
Increasingly, however, there is no money to
do that. Instead, planning departments have
become involved in the allocation of block
grant monies from the federal government, in
revenue sharing and, more and more, in programs and criteria set up for the allocation
of those funds.

Many planning departments have another function, called master plan referrals, which
basically means that if there is any public
improvement such as a street widening, a new
public building, or the leasing or sale of
a public building, the planning department
should decide whether that action is in concert
with its master plan. This is an effectuation
tool, really, a kind of check, to tell elected
officials whether or not the actions they are about
about to take are consistent with the general
plan.

In many cities, planning departments are also
involved in historic preservation. That
function may well relate to arts programs in
the sense of finding uses that may help to
preserve fine old buildings. The South San
Francisco Opera House in San Francisco was
about to be torn down some years ago, but was
saved largely through the efforts of the city's

political pressures so that they could take a long view in their deliberations about the future of the city. The obvious criticism of this arrangement is that it takes the planners out of the mainstream of politics and lets them serve in a merely advisory capacity.

Since 1940 the tendency has been to put planning directly under the chief executive. This approach, too, has drawbacks. For instance, planning in medium- and small-sized cities is often under a city manager. City managers are seldom strong supporters of city planning. Their basic goal is to balance the budget. In larger cities planners would be directly under the mayor, but if you think about those who are elected mayors of major American cities and ask if they are planning oriented, you may be somewhat disheartened.

What exactly do planners do? In most cities the city planning agency is mandated to carry out certain formal responsibilities. Almost every planning agency is responsible for preparing and keeping current a master plan or general plan for the city as a whole. This comprehensive, long-range plan usually addresses the questions of what should go where, why, how and when, in relation to the people who live and work in the city and in relation to the environment--the physical environment related to people, but still the physical environment.

At this point, a question might be: Is planning for the arts usually a part of this general plan in any conscious way? The reality is that it is usually not. General public facilities planning does come under master planning for the city, but is usually limited to major public facilities. There may be arts facilities associated with a major civic center, for instance, but the focus is not apt to be on the arts facilities themselves.

planning department, which knew where to get
money and how to find someone to use it. The
use to which the structure was put included a
major neighborhood arts program.

Another major function of planning agencies
is zoning, the use of police power to protect
health, safety and welfare. Rooted in nuisance
abatement laws, this function involves the
creation of zones that dictate what can go
where, including not only the height of buildings, but also the activities and facilities
associated with those buildings, including
those related to the arts. Arts activities
are generally permitted in all except residential zones. In some areas they are restricted
by what is called conditional-use zoning. Conditional uses are those which might be suitable
in any given zone if they meet certain criteria.
The criteria in many cities are that the use
must be "needed" and must enhance the area.

Many planning departments are also responsible
for something called variances. Under some
hardships or very special circumstances, a use
that isn't otherwise permitted is allowed. The
needs of artists as working people in the
community may come into focus when they call
for variance from zoning laws that will not
permit residential use in industrial zones.
The use of old loft buildings for combined living/
workspaces for artists, often in industrial areas,
is seldom permitted under standard zoning laws.
This is beginning to change, however, often
through the use of variances or conditional-use
zoning. Thus, some headway is being made.

Briefly, that is who city planners are and
those are a few of the many things that they
do. Most of the things that they do are not
directly related to the arts or to artists.
As the arts become a larger part of the life of
cities, so will they become a larger part of
city planning.

Arts Amenities in Comprehensive Plans

by R. Gene Brooks
Associate Dean, School of Architecture and Environmental Design, University of Texas at Arlington

In discussing arts and amenities in relation to the comprehensive plan, I define that "plan" not in its traditional terms of maps, statistics, or documentation, but in broader terms of community and arts of the people.

I hope to show, first, that the comprehensive plan is no more effective than the process, that in that process is the opportunity for the arts community to engage the people, and therein lies its strength; second, that the process means an involvement with the people in order to insure the plurality of expression so crucial to making the arts of the people; third, that there is a growing need for people to express themselves, that "the system," especially in the cities, often retards those wants; and finally, that we must begin to break down some of the barriers that exist between the arts and the people--barriers not necessarily consciously erected but which must be recognized before we can hope to build a broader base of people involved in the arts.

To accomplish these objectives we must first recognize that a strong public role in and commitment to the arts and amenities through planning is essential. Many cities and certainly the suburbs are good examples of this cultural neglect. Without the public's input in defining the areas, elements, amenities, and programs of the community, the whole act of participating in the arts is frustrated.

We must recognize, too, that the public has an
obligation to the silent minority; that people
want an opportunity to express themselves and
to seek the refuge of a quiet park and are
willing to pay for it. People want to participate in the process. Everyone wants to
belong, and many are going to great lengths to
show us they need a mechanism and opportunity
for self-expression.

First, in an attempt to eliminate some of the
vagaries associated with this topic, I think
it appropriate to define for our purposes the
term *amenities*.

The mention of amenities in the city often
conjures up a visual image of some superfluous
embellishments to the urban environment, such
as plazas, parks, band shelter, fountains,
sculptures, or supergraphics. More often than
not these conform to the definition as "a
feature conducive to attractiveness and value."
Although the initial thought is of some decorative
entity in the landscape, almost without exception
these embellishments have come to be thought of
as positive, important, and essential components
of the city. The though of urban places devoid
of such "amenities" and replaced by office
buildings, parking lots, roads or subdivisions,
makes even the most conservative individual
shudder.

There is a blur between the notion of a non-
essential amenity and that which we know begins
to make the city humane. There is an indisputable
relationship between the humane quality of an
environment and the quality of its amenities.
While we use the word to imply something superfluous, the point is that we know amenities
to be an essential aspect in a human environment.
As a practical matter, society does not accept
life completely devoid of amenities. Swimming

pools, golf courses, television sets, campers,
vans, trash compactors, electric blankets, and
a kaleidoscope of electronic gadgetry represent
common elements in our daily lives that must
be considered something above a spartan
existence.

An unfortunate prevailing attitude, however
hostile, accepts the city as someone else's
responsibility and that embellishment--whether
plaza, sculpture, or landscaping--is somehow a
questionable use of the city treasury. Our
creed of "every man for himself" has encouraged
individual acquisitions to the general demise
of our collective contribution to a community
spirit. The exceptional cases where an
attitude of community prevails are probably
most visable in some of our "new towns."

I was a resident of the new town, Reston, Virginia,
for almost six years, and it was readily obvious
that the town's amenities were not only valuable
resources for residents, but that Reston could
become a model for other communities. I
believe no small part of the success of this
community can be attributed to the extent and
quality of its amenities. The knowledge
that this was a special place was infectious.
Adults as well as children knew this place was
unique, and this knowledge translated into
pride, caring and civic participation difficult
to match.

The inner city has had its own set of problems
separate and distinct from the suburbs. Historically, the city has not enjoyed wide public
acceptance and has for the most part been a home
only for those who could afford little else.
The real expression of community, and certain
art, in the city was suppressed, with only modest
monuments surfacing as tributes to heroes or

martyrs. This followed very closely the philosophy of Thomas Jefferson, who envisioned the new republic without icons of any leader.

As a young country with an upwardly mobile society, America formed a value system focused upon individual economic achievements which did little to foster our collective contributions to community. This was not a case of "either/or," but reflected an accepted popular ethic of rugged individualism. Community spirit in America did not thrive until the "city beautiful" movement of the late nineteenth century. The planning of Daniel Burnam and Fredrick Olmstead gave focus and attention to the city as a form and identified the public sector as a client with specific aesthetic considerations. The idea was radically different from the precepts accepted in that era, as the term "city beautiful" was an obvious departure from actual conditions of the time: "city ugly."

Although the Depression caused a major setback in the development of the "city beautiful" concept, the Works Progress Administration (WPA) and other New Deal programs provided some outlet for such expression. And in later years, the concept re-emerged in the expression of Art Nouveau and Art Deco. The United States had no sooner righted an economically disastrous depression than we found ourselves engaged in another conflict. As our attention--appropriately--was focused on world crisis, World War II dissolved any potential expression of "plurality" in society. Only recently has the possibility again emerged for the city as an expression of high cultural achievement.

The past thirty years of America's history may very well be our longest uninterrupted length of general economic prosperity without preoccupation with either civil strife or international conflict. We now have the energy and time to look at ourselves, to listen to each other, to understand who we are and from where we came. The fruits of this introspection are surfacing in every art form. Our wider acceptance of art in its many configurations today would have been considered radical and outrageous by even the most avant-garde twenty years ago.

The French philosopher Sylvere Lotringer has implied that this tolerance is no small phenomenon. He suggests that America is probably one of the few remaining nations in which absolute freedom of expression, aloof from a political process and practiced by a plural, democratic constituency, is permitted and exercised. In such freedom we have come to recognize, and exemplify, the significance of our unique historical context.

Part of our communal self-awareness is our sense of what art means to us. Traditionally, art has been reviewed and dealt with in a variety of ways. If the artwork is conventional, it is often collected and locked away in a museum. Or it becomes an object structure that stands, often awkwardly, in front of the city hall, a bank, library or in some nondescript public space. If it is unconventional, the art object must often withstand strong public scrutiny and is sometimes labeled with two common synonyms: strange or weird.

The business community has emerged as a highly significant supporter of community arts endeavors. Surmounting conventional views of art, some in the business sector understand well the advantages of amenities in the physical environment. Participation in the arts by several businessmen has proved important aesthetically as well as financially.

One such businessman is Ray Nasher, developer
of the North Park Shopping Center in Dallas.
Nasher has apparently always had a continuing
concern for the aesthetic climate of Dallas as
well as the other cities in which he had projects.
This concern earned him the Businessman in
the Arts Award in 1976. Nasher was fortunate
in his choice of North Park, where a great deal
of money goes to arts-related activities as
well as to expensive programs for music, sculpture, dance, theatre, and painting. Unfortunately, despite the city's great efforts at
pre-planning and coordination, there is still
little community participation in the arts,
except in programs which are totally structured.

A recent example of an attempt to involve the
public with art is the "Running Fence" of
Christo Jovacheff. This canvas "fence" or
"ribbon" running through the California
countryside has been described by art critic
Michele Cone as "a madman's poetic vision."
Christo's initial idea was that, for two
weeks, people driving through Sonoma and
Marin Counties, California, could have an
occasional glimpse at an eighteen-foot-high,
twenty-four-mile-long "wall" running amid grazing
cattle, cresting at a hill, approaching the road,
stopping and starting again on the other side, and
finally reappearing in the distance, from behind
a clump of trees. The "fence," changing in
topography and landscape, came to be an integrated kinetic experience.

Not only was the project an aesthetic event
for the motorist, but it became an aesthetic
experience for a particular group of people
who had never before been confronted with or
understood modern art. This stems from Christo's
feeling that there is an important process both
in financing and in erecting art that involves
the community as a whole. The "fence" was not

financed by a federal grant, but by Christo
himself, through the selling of sketches of
the piece to the fifty-nine landowners on whose
land the "fence" would stand. The owners lived
in an area with particularly stringent zoning
laws and delicate ecology. The total enterprise involved the efforts of thousands of
people. As explained by art critic Marina
Vaizey, "These human collaborators, willing or
unwilling, were part of what Christo sees as
art. Anyone who has participated, from
journalists to judges, has been in some way
part of Christo's social culture."

To Christo, the point of "Running Fence" seems
to be the "amplification of our own responses."
This amplification, of course, is due both to
the fence and the land which it augments. As
Christo noted, "Those dusty brown fields, the
cows, sheep, horses, the sea, the sky, green
groves of eucalyptus, the people--this amplification is, of course, the prime purpose of
art, a purpose too often abandoned and forgot-
ten in the jargon in which we surround its
direct experience."

Christo has been offered other opportunities
to create on private property, which would
mean no difficulties with public authorities,
but he has declined. It is "the public process
and debate" that is important to him.

What is interesting is that "Running Fence"
eventually became a true community event.
Marina Vaizey observed that Christo involved
"ranchers, post office attendants, fire chiefs,
and environmentalists, all of whom became friends
because of Christo's ability to rally members
of society who are not particularly receptive
to modern art." Here is a case, then, where the
process of community involvement made the artwork purposeful and even understandable.

Attempts are emerging in other communities at
environmental arts, but frustrations are pro-
lific because of the ambiguity inherent in
defining the "values" of the participants.
Planners took quite some time to acknowledge
that this excruciating ritual was as arduous
for doctor as it was for patient. While that
may be an elaboration of the obvious, the
definition of a strong middle-class attitude
toward the arts may still be in the nineteenth
century.

Why? For an answer, let us examine the way three
of the elements I discussed earlier--art, arts
in the community, and arts in the business com-
munity--were merged in the city of Houston.

The Houston National Bank commissioned seven
Texas artists to design paintings to be enlarged
and transposed by professional sign painters
to billboards that lined Houston's Loop 610.
In an interview, one of the seven artists
explained, "The bank's purpose was two-fold:
first, they were doing it for their own benefit
(advertisement, promotion, etc.) and second,
to provide something of value in terms of art."

Surely one must ask, "Of what real artistic
value have the painted billboards become to
the people?" Aren't they a reflection, if not
an encouragement of the city's already flim-
flam, Saran Wrap mentality? Is this for real?
If the billboards were in a gallery, should I
use a windshield as a frame of reference?
How is a series of billboards really acknowledging
the kinetic experience of driving or was that
ever a design consideration? Here again, an
excellent opportunity was lost due to the lack
of a viable public role that could have facil-
itated the bank's desire to assist the community.

I am not criticizing the emphasis placed on
plurality of expression, but the whole situation
in Houston was so barren that there were few
opportunities for the bank to contribute in
a way that would give them the visibility they
felt necessary for their image. There should
be little wonder as to why.

If Houston is a model of economic success
(nothing succeeds like excess), it is certainly
the leading example of the philosophy that
expresses "anti-community." While the city
has an economic record that is envied by most
American cities, it ranks a shocking 140th
nationally in the amount of park acreage per
person. Mr. James Hart, director of the parks
and recreation program in Houston, has said
"Throw a dart at the map and any place it hits,
we need a park." Under the rationale of flood
control, the Corps of Engineers scathed the
banks of almost every bayou and glazed the
realigned water courses with concrete. The
now-antiseptic quality of one of that region's
most valuable natural resources provides only
the most modest opportunity for active or passive recreation. The city of Houston was not
concerned with a quality of life, but rather a
quantity of dollars. Since there was no planning, no process, no controlling mechanisms,
what feeble opportunities that did exist for the
quality of the city's life were lost between
trips to the deposit window.

Make no mistake about my criticism. I believe
the visable landscape of Houston is an indict-
ment of a local government that abdicated its
public responsibility to the private sector,
and the costs of that indifference are now
surfacing. The most unfortunate aspect of
this situation is the extraordinary opportunity
that has been lost. Had the city committed
itself to a program that reflected its various

cultural and ethnic enclaves, that acknowledged
the importance of open space acquisition, and
that sought to preserve the quality of the natural
environment, what a city is could have been!

The city of San Antonio, Texas, on the other
hand, provides quite a different model. The
contrasts between the values of the people,
their preference for a quality of life, and
their commitment to excellence are obvious.
One of the most crucial aspects of community
arts programs is participation by the community
in the planning process. Planners have for
some time widely pronounced that one of the
crucial aspects of comprehensive planning is the
process, believing that recognition of the
dynamics of the endeavor would permit a broader
understanding by society of issues and alternative
Seeking to be more socially relevant, the process
worked at encouraging wider citizen involvement to evoke a plurality of views and opinion.

Participation in the arts, however, has historically been a rather "impersonal" experience.
"We" as audience, viewer, or critic never
really participated, but remained mere voyeurs.
The closest group participation has come to
being a personal experience is probably exemplified in the music festival or an occasional
outdoor art fair. We applaud the star and
fantasize about being musicians or artists,
but we never really have an opportunity to
fulfill that need for expression.

Recently, however, the entire concept of public participation has been changing. I am not
sure whether it started with barn dancing,
county fairs, folk music festivals, or the
Mardi Gras, but people enjoy participating.
The feeling of belonging, for a moment, to
an experience larger than life is exhilarating.
One example of such participation is the rock

concert--the film *Woodstock* was more about the
audience than the musicians. The now-popular
disco is another example where each participant
has the opportunity to be the show and the star.

What is interesting in both these cases, however,
is the absence of public involvement in the process, almost never acting as sponsor and seldom
as catalyst. Our hang-ups on what is "good taste"
or "culturally important" often stifle the entire
process of such participation.

Now, however, all frustrated participants of the
art world have carte blanche to become the "Big
Event" with the opening of the film, *The Rocky
Horror Picture Show*. With this movie has come
the greatest audience involvement the film industry has ever seen. In contrast to past movie
viewing "techniques," which include sitting quietly
in our seats, occasionally gripping the armrest, or
perhaps laughing out loud, *Rocky Horror* becomes almost a straight man for the viewer.

Who started it? And why? The first audience reaction to the film occurred in a theatre in Los Angeles. The reason for the participation has been
questioned, and speculation is that the first responses came because of a certain possessive quality the audience had developed toward the film. It
was "theirs," their discovery, and therefore fos-
tered a much more personal attitude than most audiences have toward other films.

Initially, the audience began by singing with the
movie. This has now evolved to a full-fledged performance in the aisles, with a completely organized
program that the audience executes simultaneously
with the movie. The huge audiences, and the popularity of the movie, can be attributed principally
to the opportunity for participation. While many
attend *Rocky Horror* just to see the audience perform, one realizes also that the lines of people

are there, weekend after weekend, because of the opportunity to become part of the show.

The Los Angeles opening of *Rocky Horror* in 1975 was a colossal failure. The producers then decided that they would have to use some psychology to promote the movie. The approach they devised was not to advertise in the normal fashion, but to let the people "discover" the film. Tim Reegan, the film's advertising man, has conceded that hype is not always the answer. While you can sell almost anything with hype, letting people discover something for themselves is far more permanent.

The question in everyone's mind is, "Why this movie?" The answer, of course, is that the quality of the film has very little to do with its success. It is a "B" movie, accompanied by poor writing and equivalent acting. It is the audience's role that makes *Rocky Horror* one of the most talked about public events both abroad and in the United States.

Film critic, Keith Mano, describes the scene in front of the theatre hours before show time:

"At 11 pm, an hour before curtain, the line has already elled itself off Queen's Boulevard, north-northwestward. About three dozen or so veterans of the long-run engagement are grunting into costumes; boys with Dr. Frank N. Furter pantyhose and bra-corsets, in white face and lipstick, girls wit the same. A baldhead skullcap wig for those who will play Riffraff; eyeshadow and motorcycle greas for the Meatloaves. Each has chosen to typecast him/herself in a single role. They can mime and dub every phoneme, gesture, eyebrow hitch-up. Practice makes perfervid."

Some have been to the movie 100 to 200 times. The costumes are duplicated with accuracy; viewers flawlessly lip-sync and act out the movie on theatre stages and in the aisles. If one audience character is doing a solo, twenty to thirty BIC lighters emerge from the audience to create the proper lighting effect. During the movie's "Time Warp" dance, where a crowd of Transylvanians dances to the tune, the audience "transylvanians" stream out into the aisles to mimic those on the screen. While the audience role began simply as song and dance routines, a whole dialogue has developed for audience use in response to the film.

William Henkins, author of *The Rocky Horror Picture Show Book*, brings up an interesting point about *Rocky Horror*'s success:

"There is an odd kind of camaraderie practiced here, just perfect for the seventies. Fast-food intimacy; a burger jack and a small order of... Whoopie! I'm wearing a garter belt! A large coke and an apple pie filled with...'Look, Ma! I'm yelling and throwing stuff!' Fun? You bet! I think I'll be a girl tonight! Hey, that's great! I'll be a guy! Take a walk on the wild side."

Keith Mano has said, "*The Rocky Horror* cult foretells a new art coming, or at least a renegotiation of terms. Public access television and call-in radio have already conceded it. Audiences want more credit, more input--equal billing at least-- or they'll go into open competition. How much of this is due to the void left by the Vietnam/Watergate crowd confrontations and the myths of that era? Chicago in 1968 was certainly a performance; Sam Brown had his groupie crew and anyone could get on television then. If it isn't Ted Mack Amateur Hour, it can at least be the Gong Show." Since we recognize that people are and want to be part of the event, how do we get from here to there?

We are all annoyed by lecturers, generals, and especially academicians that espouse: "Go forth and feed the multitudes with three Big Macs and an order of fries," or "Improve the lot of many and transfer this ugly mess into a Utopian vision.

Call me only if you have difficulty with these instructions."

A plan's implementation, more often than not, is its weakest link. And obviously a plan without a method for implementation is little more than a wish.

Implementation is by no means the simplest function in the urban planning process, but it should be no more difficult than other functions. The traditional methods of implementing a comprehensive city plan have been the capital improvement program and the zoning ordinance.

The zoning ordinance has been blamed for every major planning fiasco, including the lack of a national urban growth policy, since the ink was dry on the Euclid vs. Ambler Realty decision. In its defense, I believe this method was nothing more than a beginning and should not have been considered as anything more. Further, any tool used for the wrong purposes will have less than perfect results. As an example of such improper use, a study conducted in Dallas in 1974 documented the zoning holding capacity at 497 million square feet of office space at a potential density of 33 percent higher than midtown Manhattan. For a built form of approximately twenty million square feet, that is a lot of slack in a system that was ostensibly inaugurated to control land use. Obviously there must be alternatives.

Planned Unit Developments (PUD) are one of the best methods to critique and assess what the public wants on the ground. PUD's can be developed not just as density control methods, but with incentives to garner those amenities that cannot be identified through traditional prescriptive Euclidian zoning. In the words of the Rolling Stones "You can't always get what you want, but if you try sometimes you just might find, you get what you need."

Where applicable, either conditional zoning or easement in perpetuity are also tools that can be used to acquire that element crucial to the plan.

No one can discuss implementation without funding. This is one of the most crucial issues to resolve. And certainly one of the most important resources to consider is the financial support available at the federal level through numerous programs developed by the National Endowment for the Arts (NEA), the National Endowment for the Humanities (NEH), and now the Comprehensive Employment and Training Act (CETA). These programs offer a range of opportunities for local governments as well as individuals to prepare programs, seminars, exhibits, or films on a wide range of issues. There are direct grants, matching grants or challenge grants available.

In addition to these NEA, NEH and CETA grants, substantial financial assistance can come from local government. The first and most obvious form of assistance is municipal bonds. Then there are three rather more obscure alternatives. One is the special taxing district. This is a method whereby an entity collectively decides it wants to inaugurate a self-imposed tax. The best example is from the "new town" of Reston. The citizens believed a community center was needed, but were without any governing mechanism as the "town" had no jurisdictional authority within the county. After consideration of the request, Fairfax County decided the project could not be financed through normal funding procedures. The alternative was a self-imposed tax upon each household in the community. The fee was a nominal annual contribution to finance the initial construction and pay the monthly mortgage notes. The concept is rather simple and, legislation permitting, can be used to acquire an open space, finance lighting for a

pedestrian system, or sustain a program of
baroque music.

The second rather obscure means of financial
assistance is the real estate transfer tax.
This taxing method can be an incredible financial boon to an area that is growing. The state
of Maryland may still, as they did at one time,
use this mechanism. Just as there is a sales
tax on other items sold in the state, there is
a tax on property as well; but in this case the
one receiving the money pays. For example, there
may be a sales tax of one-tenth of one percent
levied on the seller of any real estate that
changes hands. While one-tenth of one percent
is not much in itself, when collected from many
land transactions over a long period of time, the
income can be significant. The state of Maryland
worked out a program of returning those transfer
tax funds to the local jurisdictions through a
formula based on population, contribution to the
program, and need for the acquisition of open
space. I must point out, however, that the real
estate lobby will likely fight any such program
with every resource available to them.

In closing it seems to me essential that planners
bear the following in mind: Without the entire
community participating in the process with some
specific objectives, the process gets very frus-
trating. From time to time your council will
suggest that they have been elected and can speak
for the people. I suggest that the people can
speak for themselves, and I hope that I have convinced you that they have gone to some pretty
unusual extremes to tell us.

Second, a word to the arts community. The process
often appears circuitous and requires a certain
patience. Look for opportunities to contribute.
One example is the Torpedo Factory in Alexandria,
Virginia. A remnant of World War II, it was a

massive, dull hulk that was functionally an eye-
sore. In 1973, the community began looking for
a viable use for the building shell. The possibility emerged of converting the entire space to
studios and leasing those studios to painters,
sculptors, weavers, potters, photographers, and
other artists, and it became operational in 1974.
The Torpedo Factory Arts Center is now the key-
stone in a major revitalization effort in that
city.

Finally, it is impossible to realize the potential of a community without working for change.
Failure is not in our inability to affect change,
but in the absence of an attempt to change. The
quality of our society can only be elevated when
the opportunity for an expression of its visions
can be shared.

The Arts and Economic Development

by Louise Wiener
Special Assistant for Cultural Resource Development, U.S. Department of Commerce

I want to comment first on the relevance of
planning to the arts community from the point
of view of economic development and what I
think that requires from the arts community
to make it effective. Secondly, I would like
to discuss how the programs of the Economic
Development Administration (EDA) and other
federal agencies can be leveraged with that
effective planning.

At EDA we refer not to the arts but to
cultural resources, and cultural resources
by our definition include the profit and nonprofit activities of the arts, humanities and
historic preservation. We perceive cultural
resources to include two categories: One is
the arts and humanities institutions themselves,
and the other deals with such elements as design,
historic preservation, adaptive re-use, and
beautification. The two frequently come together,
and they are generally complementary, but they
do not have to come together. It is important,
I think, to know the difference between the
two categories and which one you are discussing.

I had several meetings over the past few days
with the historic preservation people, and one
of the issues that they were dealing with was
the fact that very often the preservationist
approach is perceived as being obstructionist.
The preservationist comes in and says, "Don't
tear it down. Save this; it's valuable. It's
culturally valuable, it's artistically valuable.
We should hold on to it." It might as easily be

said that the arts community is also approaching
planning issues from a somewhat obstructionist
point of view. That is, more, "What should the
planners not be doing and how do we stop them
from doing the wrong thing and make them take
us into account?" as opposed to, "How do we work
with this system to make it sensitive to our
needs and to the assets which we can bring to
their initiatives and their concerns?"

Within that context, then, how do we begin?
After all, so much is going on that we want to
stop. I am reminded of a story about some gentle-
men who were fishing. They had a lovely afternoon
and, just when the afternoon was about over, they
saw a child floating down the river. They pulled
the child out and were in the process of taking
care of that child when they saw another child.
And more and more children were coming down the
river. The fishermen called for help and people
came to the river and began pulling out the children as fast as they were coming in. Suddenly
one of the fishermen started to leave. The others
shouted, "Hey, wait a minute. Where are you going?
There are more kids coming down the river." He
said, "You stay here and pull them out. I'm
going upstream to find out who's throwing them
in." I think that is where we in arts and city
planning need to be. We need to go upstream to
find out how this system begins.

The basic tool the arts community needs to really
effect a planning system is an inventory, an
assessment of its own values and its own objectives. Part one of the inventory should include
culturally or historically relevant buildings
around the city, both abandoned and active ones,
and a listing of the city's open spaces. We are
talking about a physical inventory, sites in which
you are interested. It is very important to make
a distinction in the inventory between register-
eligible buildings, in the sense of formal historic

preservation, and the more general preservation concept, where you have lovely buildings in which the community has an investment and really wants to see saved, but are not register-eligible.

The second part of the inventory should assess the needs and opportunities represented by the cultural institutions looking for space. Is a need for space one of your issues? What do you need to develop your "market" further, expand your audience, expand your services? To what extent does your need reflect an opportunity for the urban planner and economic developer?

The third category of the inventory is cultural activities. This should include both cultural institutions, such as museums, symphony, theatre, etc., as well as crafts, folklore, folkways, ethnic neighborhood activities, etc. At the core of the rationale for such an assessment is the understanding that cultural activity is a people-magnet, that is, a generator for activity. That generator may be just what the urban planner is looking for, because that kind of vitality then creates an environment which may indeed be more conducive to business development, to tourism development, to attracting and retaining residents.

The classic example of this generator concept is Lincoln Center, which demonstrated that you could take a relatively forlorn redevelopment area, infuse cultural activity, and around that activity create a kind of economic vitality and desirability that's really second to none. But it need not be Lincoln Center, a major institution. New York's 42nd Street redevelopment project is a consortium of small, experimental groups with a wide range of activities. Or one can leave New York and go to a very rural environment like Mountain View, Arkansas with its Ozark Cultural Center. Or one can look at a small town like Greenville, South

Carolina and find that craft activities, craft
lessons, drama classes, community theatre, etc.,
are being placed in the Main Street area and
are beginning to turn Main Street around. It
is no longer a place without a reason for being
and without an attraction to the population as
a whole.

Therefore, if you can convince your community that
the people-magnet concept will help stimulate
other objectives and will also expand the audience for the arts activities themselves, you
now have a trading tool. Now you need to know,
what are the target areas for these urban planners?
Where are they? For what are they looking? Obviously I come at this from the point of view of
their economic development objectives, because
that is the area with which I deal. But I believe
that the same kind of thing could be related to
the housing issue or the transportation issue.

How many times have cultural activities been
placed in areas where the only access is by
automobile? And what kind of financial situation will that put the cultural institutions in
over the next few years? There is, within the
Federal Council on the Arts and Humanities, an
Energy Task Force, which is currently looking at
two issues: one, the energy needs of cultural
institutions, and how existing programs can deal
with those needs; and two, transportation
planning. The task force noted, for instance,
that during the energy crisis this past summer,
museum attendance soared because most museums
are downtown and easily accessible by public
transportation. Inner city arts activities
responded effectively in providing constructive
activity when a lack of gasoline precluded
extensive travel.

Thus, there are many elements which are traditionally city planners' concerns where the arts have

an opportunity to say, "We can help you with this
or we can help you with that," and helping them
is helping you. This can be a pretty even exchange if done well. But it is absolutely critical that you not go to the planners with only a
generalized concept that because the arts represent the most humane and sensitive elements of our
society, it is the planner's responsibility to do
something more and better than they have done before
I suspect most of them would agree with you. But
to gain their support you must have something more
meaningful to back it with: "I have some places
to begin....I have some information you weren't
aware of..."

Michael Pittas, director of the Design Arts
Program for the National Endowment for the Arts,
said it very succinctly: "The value to the arts
community of this planning process is access to
more large grant money." What we are really
trying to do in this process is dip into other
tills and to do it in a legitimate way. I
think this is significant primarily because if
the past few years have been at all indicative
of what's coming, the growth in funding for
cultural resources is not likely to come through
cultural dollars per se, but in expanded access
to all the other kinds of major grants categories,
And, without planning tools, we simply are not
going to know how to get at those other dollars.

One particularly useful tool for gaining access
to grant money is to know where "designated
areas" are. Economic Development Administration
dollars and Department of Housing and Urban
Development dollars are not going just anywhere;
they are going to designated areas, and those
areas are designated on two bases, unemployment
rates and levels of income. To best qualify for
facilities grants, you want to be in an area that
the city has designated as a prime target, because
the direct grant opportunity is dependent in most

instances on the priority that the cities put on the project. Before you get discouraged, let me tell you that in 1978 EDA spent approximately $15 million on cultural facilities, in 1979 approximately $30 million, and in 1980 appears likely to spend nearly twice the fiscal year 1979 appropriation. This means that when you know where you are going and why you are going there, it is not impossible to get on that priority list.

There is some irony in the fact that larger cities, with potentially the largest number of opportunities for cultural resources to gain priority status, also have the largest number of demands on economic development money. In a sense it seems harder to make the case in big cities than in smaller ones. Although New York City has taken the lead in many things, it has not been effective in getting grant monies for cultural facilities. I suspect that reflects the huge demand on development dollars in a city of that size. But I also find this situation is often due to how active the arts community has been and to how well its efforts have been coordinated with the planning and economic development activities of a city.

I would like to discuss, at this point, a new proposed program in the department that may be of particular interest to large city institutions. In the pending legislation, the loan and loan guarantee program of EDA is projected to become a major program. The loan guarantee program is projected in the legislation at $1.8 billion, and the direct loan program is projected at about $300 million. This new initiative, called the Development Financing Program (DFP), is a major expansion of the existing business loan and loan guarantee program.

The difference between public works grants and the business loan and loan guarantee opportunities is basic. In the direct grants program, the city sets the priority level. All applications must relate to the overall economic development plan, and it is your priority level on that plan that is going to decide whether or not you receive funding. With the business loan and loan guarantee program, the private sector has the dominant role. Certainly a city sign-off is required which says that the initiative this private group sector wants to undertake is in concert with the overall economic development plan. But it is essentially a private sector initiative. With the loan guarantee situation, the EDA can potentially guarantee up to 90 percent of the eligible parts of the loan. The eligible part of the loan may be 100 percent and the way of determining that is through the jobs created to dollars spent ratio.

Guidelines and regulations for the projected new legislation may give that job to dollars ratio a little more flexibility than before. Questions are continually raised about separate guidelines and/or designated pots of money for cultural resources. My recommendation is to structure the guidelines and regulations to be flexible enough to broaden the access of cultural institutions, but I am wary of establishing a separate category. I also do not want a separate category because it puts a cap on how much money will be spent. Once you have a separate category, you can be told specifically to spend this much and no more. I can assure you that if we had gone for a special program in fiscal year 1978 or 1979, nobody would have agreed to the numbers that, in fact, we spent.

The arts community needs to think about this long and hard, because a lot of energy goes into fighting for targeted money. The targeted money is always small, and it never begins to scratch the surface of the needs that you have. Therefore, I urge you to look at infiltrating the big money that is there by thoroughly planning to make better and better use of that money.

The budget projections in the new legislation suggest a combined loan and loan guarantee capacity of $2 billion. The minimum loan is $500,000. How can loans and loan guarantees be used by the cultural community? Loans imply that they have to be repaid. Frankly, my recommendation would be to really look at those opportunities that can expand the earned income base of the institution with which you are concerned. That may mean expanding the museum shop and restaurant service at the same time that you expand the exhibition facilities of the museum.

Or it may mean making better use of deeded pieces of property that were bequests from major donors. Often these properties have not been income-producing because nobody could afford to renovate the property for a new use. There is a great opportunity to turn this into an income-producing space, even as a rental space for small businesses, with the cultural institution taking out the development loan for the refurbishing of the real estate, and then allowing the income from that real estate to support the cultural institution.

The wide variety of ways to use these funds is limited only by two things: one, your own imagination and, two, your candid evaluation of whether or not there is a built-in repayment capacity. Remember, the projected loan and loan guarantee program is useful to large institutions because of the $500,000 minimum.

There is, in addition, a smaller loan program, which might be of great interest to smaller organizations, known as the revolving loan fund. This fund is awarded directly to the community, city or economic development district, and it is generally used for the needs of small business in that area, such as refurbishing, rehabilitation

and modification of buildings. The revolving loan
fund may be of particular interest to smaller community organizations, particularly arts consortia.

In closing I would like to suggest that the
economic impact statements that many of you have
done represent nothing more than the basic home-
work that you need for your own understanding.
They are by no means an end; they are the very
beginning of a tool. If you undertake one, be
sure you undertake it straight so that you have
the information that you really need to know. I
think that the economic impact statement as an
advocacy tool has done its job, to credibly
establish that the arts and cultural activities
are more than just another worthy cause.

The real economic impact statement that you
need to make is a statement of where you are,
what you have got to offer the community, how
many jobs you create, and how many additional
jobs you support in other sectors. Know where
you are--for your own information and for your
planning purposes.

Once you have that information, begin to use it
in terms of your needs for facilities. How does
that information affect your understanding of
your housing needs? Your transportation needs?
Your energy costs? Make the distinction in your
own mind between what you need to have available
to you for advocacy and what you need to have
available to you for your own planning, to assure
that you are able to work with the city, or the
economic developer, or the transportation or
housing planner as a true partner. Armed with
an adequate understanding of your own capacities
and needs, the arts community can present itself
to the economic development planner as a valuable
asset, resource, and partner in mutually reinforc-
ing initiatives.

The Arts and Urban Design

by Richard S. Weinstein
Architect, Richard S. Weinstein Associates, Inc.

Urban design is just one aspect of the design
arts which I regard as being absolutely con-
tinuous--from an individual building, however
small, to a city or a neighborhood or groups of
buildings, however large. There are, of course,
differences between architecture and city planning. But it is important to understand what is
the same about them. What is the same is that
they are both concerned with making metaphors
about the institutional life of a culture. By
metaphor I mean a poetic statement about the
relationships between persons and groups of persons in a society. Individual buildings are
about that as well as cities.

Somehow a great work of architecture from the
past seems more successful than any other art
form at capturing the essence of the civiliza-
tion in which it is placed--for example, the
Acropolis, the mediaeval cathedral, the Roman
Forum, the Renaissance city.

In the construction of a building or group of
buildings, there is an aggregate of decisions
required. Hundreds of people usually are
involved in a building project of any conse-
quence. Even the building of a house involves
contractors, engineers, architects and local
zoning boards as well as family. Thus, one
of the distinguishing characteristics of the
design arts apropos of the built environment
is that they involve institutional decisions--
hence, a great many people.

Frequently, a great deal of money is involved
in building a building or a cathedral or a

temple. This, of course, is one of the reasons
that the artistic metaphors of this form
involve large numbers of persons and institu-
tions--just because of the decision-making
process involved. When you involve the decisions of a great many persons and you spend
large amounts of money, you are dealing necessarily with the establishment of the culture
involved--an establishment by aristocracy. That
is to say, an establishment exists in a democracy
as well as it did in Renaissance Italy. The
difference is that the power to make decisions
is conferred by vote in our culture while in
other cultures it was conferred by birth or
something else.

Something rather curious happened, however,
after World War I. Up until that time there
was never any question that architects and
city planners were in the service of the establishment of the civilizations for which they
worked. We use a nice word, patrons, but
basically they were the same as the Pope or
Pericles--the ruling powers of the countries
which built the monuments we so admire. After
World War I in Europe, out of the pain and
suffering that culminated in the end of the
Industrial Revolution, European intellectuals
and artists--like most sensitive, thoughtful
people of the time--came under the influence
of Marxist teachings. Out of that milieu of
ferment came the Bauhaus, which, as World War II
approached, was transferred from Europe to
Harvard and had a major influence on nearly
two generations of architectural planners in
this country.

It is not surprising that those who were
trained at the Bauhaus came to look upon the
establishment which had produced the ruin of
Europe as corrupt, ineffective, stupid, insensi-
tive, venal. Modern architecture and city

planning as we know it and as it has affected most of our cities grew out of this perception of the artists in the design arts that they had to do battle against the Philistine establishment.

Thus, a schism developed for the first time in the history of city planning and architecture. Michelangelo didn't have any fundamental disagreements with the Pope about what constituted an orderly and just society. He just went ahead glorifying values that were generally held by most of the people in Renaissance Italy. Likewise the thousands, or hundreds of thousands, who worked over fifteen years to produce Chartres never questioned the feudal order of mediaeval Europe. However, in the last seventy years or so, those who have worked on cities and on building were nurtured with the idea that one should be suspicious of the prevailing arrangements promulgated and sustained by the establishment--whom we both hated and sought as our patrons.

That schism between the establishment and the way things were done by the profession began to fall apart ten to fifteen years ago as the modern movement began to run out of gas. Meanwhile, the American city as we know it had been built almost entirely without the benefit of the best professional and artistic talents in the country. At least 95 percent of America was not built by the heirs to the Gropius tradition at Harvard; it was built by real estate developers, lawyers and politicians who used builders and contractors but almost never used architects, or when they did use architects, almost never chose one who self-evidently had the ability to produce significant work.

We are now in what is called the post-modern era, and that schism between the establishment

and architects is being healed slowly. There
is a new wind blowing and I think it is a
healthy one. In it I see signs of a reintegra-
tion of those who hold the power to control the
construction of large physical entities--whether
groups of buildings or communities--and the
talented people who are best suited to build
them.

In the course of the past sixty years, we have
developed in some of our cities--certainly in
our major cities--a notion that uses should be
separated into a pure land-use pattern. For
instance, in one area is the business district,
in yet another the commercial district. These
separations are all commonplace to us now.
Meis van der Rohe wouldn't even allow a bank at
the base of the Seagram Building. His objective
was to surround that building with as much space
as possible so that it was perceived as an
object literally disengaged from the street.

Some of this orientation has its origins in
Cubism and some in social theory. But the
impact, of course, was the same: to destroy
the continuity and diverse uses of the street
and to begin to treat buildings as independent
of their context, exactly the way the architect
or physical designer was seen as independent
of the mainstream of society, as holding a
different vision from that mainstream. That
is all changing now, for the better.

The question, of course, arises: What is there
about our contemporary way of life that suits
itself to the making of these institutional
metaphors? One aesthetician, who prefers the
term ethnic domain to institutional metaphor,
states that the design arts somehow capture
in an intuitive way, through art, the fundamental
relationships among the working parts of a
society. Obviously a cathedral doesn't literally

define the hierarchy of feudal organization
in any discursive way, where one could say:
"There are this many peasants to this many
landowners, to this many knights, to this many
kings." But one does get an image--an aesthetic
image--of that hierarchy, building up, parti-
tioning, etc.

What is there in our culture that stands in
relation to our society in the way a cathedral
stood in relation to the Middle Ages and that
allows us a sense of what our institutions and
their relationships to one another are all
about? One institution in our culture that
lends itself to this kind of thinking is the
marketplace--the marketplace conceived of as
a mechanism for achieving value-oriented or
social goals in a pluralistic, democratic kind
of society. And, oddly enough, this is how
Jefferson viewed the business of making money.
He saw it as a means of achieving the purposes
of the Republic without resort to tyranny or
mob rule or aristocratic precedent. He makes
it clear in some of his early writings that
he regarded what I call the marketplace as the
way American society ought to do its business,
because it was a way of sorting out while providing self-determination for individuals.

By marketplace I mean commercial transactions,
but commercial transactions specifically in
relation to social goals, which are primary in
the design of the machinery of the marketplace.
Of course, the commercial marketplace is
exactly the thing Bauhaus detested because it
is essentially a middle-class operation. The
Marxists wanted to exclude the middle class
and deal exclusively with the rulers and the
proletariat--the ordinary, uneducated craftsman
united with the visionary artist in perfect
harmony building a brave new world.

Thus, the marketplace is precisely the essence
of contemporary society, at least in our country,
and to a lesser extent in Europe. Shopping
centers were built, and people began to realize
that the streets they liked best were the
streets with shops and restaurants. James
Jacobs wrote a book in which he describes
Greenwich Village and the Italian sections of
New York City as virtually the only sections
of the city that remained humane. Then Louis
Kahn came along, having somehow matured as an
architect without any apparent influence from
the Brauhaus. We have been launched into the
post-modern era.

There are two primary architectural images that
function as metaphors for this new era. One,
of course, is the downtown skyline. The skyline is a visual metaphor for the process of
the commercial marketplace. These random erup-
tions of energy and power are in the aggregate
the kind of metaphor I am talking about for
the marketplace.

The second primary image is the suburban shopping mall. An invention of the developers,
the first malls were totally unaffected by architects. Only in the last three or four years
have significant architects been commissioned
to design shopping malls.

Unnoticed until recently is the fact that the
arts have always had an effect on the marketplace in this country. Previously, just as
the development of commercial transactions in
the United States was seen to be in the service
of something higher--namely, a concept that
would allow the maximum number of people to
have the fullest life without interfering with
the pursuit of happiness for others--the arts
have historically been viewed as having an
inherent value apart from any commercial

transaction. Now, however, this additional role of art as significant to the American concept of the marketplace is being fully realized.

My argument is that the commercial mainstream is the essential organizing principle of the society we live in and that such organization was done basically for a value-oriented purpose. Thus, since the arts are obviously all about values, it follows that the integration of the arts and the commercial mainstream, rather than their separation, is something of great importance to our culture. In fact, that integration is one of the distinguishing characteristics of our culture.

How do the arts confer this kind of value? Lincoln Center in New York City serves as a good example. Development around Lincoln Center has already paid for the center itself ten times over. Lincoln Center cost $140 million when it was built. Additional tax revenue from buildings built around Lincoln Center is estimated to be $30 million a year. So that is one simple way of measuring the marketplace value of Lincoln Center: $30 million a year. The principle is a basic one. Build Lincoln Center and you have thousands of people going there--people who want to eat, drink, shop. The twenty blocks of Columbus Avenue north of Lincoln Center now have a totally different retail character which can be tied directly to the influence of Lincoln Center.

There are examples in Baltimore, Boston and elsewhere that the arts improve the character of downtown areas. There is a complex interaction, a complex social and cultural ecology, among the popular arts, the commercial arts, the fine arts and the marketplace. An

institutional web ties the advertising artist
to Frank Sinatra to the record company to
Luciano Pavarotti to new opera, and so on.

It is important that we understand those
institutional relationships and articulate
them, so that we know how to manipulate them
for our own purposes the way a banker or a
lawyer or a real estate developer would. We
will then be able to compete more successfully
for our own interests--one of which is a
bigger share of the marketplace for the arts.

The marketplace, broadly conceived, is the
machinery for creating and exchanging ideas,
and for doing the work of society. It is
exactly that institutional web--the relationship between the lawyer, the legislator, the
businessman, the banker--that the urban
designer has to understand. This web should
be analogued with the feudal system of the
Middle Ages. It is the system out of which
our architectural metaphors should arise and,
in fact, are arising right under our noses.
Their reality, however, has never been trans-
formed by our greatest artists into something
enriched with the kind of spiritual content
that the arts can bring. There is no reason
that a shopping center or an office building
can't be a glorious work of art. In fact,
there is every reason for that to happen, and
it is beginning to happen.

But first the arts community must learn to
view developments in media and communications
technology not with trepidation, but with the
same vision with which the automobile lobby,
for instance, viewed the Highway Trust Fund.
The automobile lobby built this country's
system of roads primarily from gasoline taxes,
and in its wake produced the Federal Insurance
Program and single-family housing. This,

combined with the value-oriented desire of
politicians to give something to the World
War II veterans, created the suburban structure
of this country.

Arts-related people should be looking to cable
television, video discs, all of the explosions
that are going to happen in the next thirty years
in the communications and computer industries,
because these people will be the source of the
software--the plays, the ballets, the music--
that the mass media need. People who are serious
about the arts are going to have to understand
the technology and the workings of the computer
and communications industries if they want to get
their share of the action.

As I learned when I worked as a commissioner of
development, unless I could play the lawyer's
game, the real estate developer's game, the
banker's game, I couldn't achieve my purposes--
which had nothing to do with money, but which
had to do with the shape the city would take.
The means to get what I wanted was to understand those institutional levers and their relationships. The arts community must do the same
thing vis a vis mass media and cable in order
to get what it wants and needs.

The development of 42nd Street in New York City
is, in its own naive and incomplete way, an
effort to understand a series of institutional
relationships within that city. The 42nd Street
project is attempting to achieve a value-
oriented purpose: the creation of a complex
that would be responsive to the needs of the
city, would incorporate the history of the
street and would also pay for itself.

One cannot be an urban designer, planner or
architect, in my opinion, without continually
integrating ideas with the question of how to make
them work--asking not what government program

will pay for this, but how the operation of
the marketplace can pay for it, without sacri-
ficing value-oriented purposes.

There is a destructive social ecology on 42nd
Street that is a national disgrace. And while
we are all responsible in a way for the social
problems concentrated on that street, there is
no need to provide a central location for their
proliferation.

There are seven subway lines at Times Square
and Seventh Avenue, another at Eighth Avenue,
a bus terminal, Pennsylvania Station one stop
away and Grand Central Terminal another stop
away. The area is the piece of urban territory
most richly served by mass transportation inter-
structure in the world. Planners have always
thought of it as the crossroads of the city--
in fact, it is nicknamed the crossroads of the
world.

Oddly, however, the biggest land use around
the Times Square area is vacant space. No
buildings are occupied over the first floor.
Many have their heating and plumbing facilities
turned off. There is water in the basements
of most.

The 42nd Street project will create two atriums:
one to the north, close in size to Grand Central
Terminal, and one to the south, built around
the shell of the Empire Theatre. The shopping
in this area will be geared to creating an international flavor. There will be a series of
neighborhoods simulating various cities of the
world--Rio, Tokyo, Paris, London--where you can
eat and buy what you would eat and buy in those
cities. The metaphor here will be the concentrated essence of "city" at the center of the
world's most important city. The third floor
of the complex will house exhibits. The

basement will have a totally reorganized Times
Square subway station as well as a series of
jazz joints and cinemas.

Ten million people are expected to come here
to shop and eat, four million to go to micro-
Broadway, ten million to commute through the
second level of the complex, above the street,
on the walkway system. Up to six million will
come to the Celebration of Cities, where for
the price of a movie ticket you can have twelve
hours of entertainment.

The precursor of this project was the Museum
of Modern Art's Condominium Tower, a project
that I developed with the same group of people
who are bringing you 42nd Street. Condominium
Tower will, in the next 30 years, be worth $75
million to the Museum of Modern Art. State
legislation was required to capture the taxes
from the commercial development to fund the
museum's expansion. We consulted with Goldman
Sachs and other financial experts on Wall Street,
and discovered half a dozen ways, because we
were a non-profit institution, to amplify the
flow of money to the museum. This is an example
of what happens if you understand the institutional arrangements of the marketplace and put
them to a value-oriented purpose.

The 42nd Street project employs basically the
same idea. Since it is an urban renewal area,
we created a not-for-profit corporation called
The City of 42nd Street, which has Harold Prince,
John Chancellor of NBC, and bankers, civic
leaders and fashion people on its board. We
are asking New York City for a lease to develop
this territory, with the right to sublease the
air space over it to commercial developers in
order to fund the entire enterprise.

Planning decisions, such as who the developer,
architect and engineer will be, are all vola-
tile political decisions because someone can
always say that there is political hanky-panky
involved. Therefore, some municipal governments, like ours, prefer to give those problems
to somebody else to handle. They create a
local development corporation and give it a
lease to build the project according to certain constraints. Then that group makes all
the decisions.

That is our current proposal to New York City--
that we become an entity which will build on
behalf of the city and make all those decisions,
decisions like whether Flo Ziegfield's old
theatre should become an American dance theatre
or an international repertory.

The 42nd Street project will offer the city
the following advantages: it will provide
$20 million in additional revenue to a city
that is near bankruptcy; it will create 15
thousand jobs; it will clean up a serious urban
blight; it will restore six of the greatest
theatres in the United States; it will present
popularly priced cultural entertainment to
6 million people a year who can't affort $20
for a theatre ticket on Broadway. The project
will do all of these things because it is
economically viable, because we already have
six of the major real estate developers on the
North American continent, including the two
biggest in Canada, willing to commit close
to $600 million of financing against $40 million
of funds we need from the federal government
to help acquire the land.

Our enterprise is sometimes viewed as a Trojan
horse, in part because it seems too good.
The question is: What's the clinker in it?

There is no clinker. The east side of Manhattan
is totally impacted with office space. The
critics are inveighing publicly in the New
York Times and elsewhere that development must
go westward, that there is no room on the
streets.

One of these critics, upon seeing this project,
asked, "But why must the commercial tail wag
the cultural dog?" That remark shows an
abysmal lack of understanding of the very
society in which that very distinguished
critic lives and functions as a critic. People
who have disciplined themselves to understand
the institutional relationships on 42nd Street
know instantly that you need the stuff in the
air (commercial development) as much as the
stuff on the ground (cultural facilities).

This interrelationship is essential because
the merging of the arts into the marketplace
process is the most effective method of planning. When New York City required proof that
our project would in no way impinge upon their
debt situation, we knew this was one way to
give them that assurance. With our 42nd Street
plan, real estate entrepreneurs are no longer
afraid to risk their assets to guarantee that
if the land is condemned, they will pay, whatever the cost. They do not expect to lose.

The Arts and Transportation

by Martin Convisser

**Director, Office of Environment and Safety,
U.S. Department of Transportation**

Transportation facilities help to shape our
urban environment. The Department of Transportation (DOT) spends more than $10 billion
annually in grants to state and local transportation agencies for the construction of transportation facilities. These agencies spend many
billions more of their own funds for transportation
construction. Daily we spend a significant
amount of time in transportation facilities, but
we do not always think about their impact on
the aesthetic aspects of our lives. Obviously
transportation has a major effect upon the
quality of life in our cities, but that effect
can be favorable or unfavorable.

Former Secretary of Transportation William
Coleman wanted the effect of transportation
upon the quality of life to be positive. In
1976, he asked a group of artists, architects,
urban planners and transportation experts to
meet with him to discuss what the department
could do to help make transportation a more
favorable influence on the aesthetics of their
cities.

That session generated some initial ideas, and
a task force was formed within the department
to review those ideas and to consider others.
The views of the general public and the arts
community were also solicited. At about the
same time, President Carter took office and made
clear his commitment to the aesthetics of urban
areas, both in his environmental message and in
his message on urban affairs.

As a result of these efforts, in September 1977
former Secretary of Transportation Brock Adams
and Mrs. Joan Mondale jointly announced a new
policy on Design, Art and Architecture in Transportation, and a series of initiatives and
programs to be implemented. The secretary
stated that the department would attempt to
improve the design quality and the artistic
quality of transportation facilities, and
announced five major initiatives to accomplish
those goals.

The five initiatives are: funding for art and
design in transportation; improved procedures
to integrate aesthetic considerations into
transportation facilities; research and training
in this field; improved graphics and transportation symbol signs; and coordination and monitoring of the overall effort.

The Department of Transportation has always,
to some extent, made funds available for
aesthetic enhancement and quality design in
transportation facilities, but the availability
of these funds was not widely known and they
were not uniformly administered throughout the
department. One of the major efforts DOT has had
underway, therefore, has been to publicize the
availability of grants for aesthetic enhancement
and design quality in federal aid transportation
projects, and to encourage the utilization of the
grant funds for this purpose.

Since that policy was announced there have
been significant accomplishments. The Urban
Mass Transit Administration (UMTA) issued a
policy statement last year permitting the use
of mass transit grant funds for art and design
in rail transit stations as well as in buses,
bus shelters and pedestrian facilities. Art
works have been included in the Atlanta subway
system and will be included in the new Baltimore

and Miami systems. "Poetry on the Buses" is another result, and the New York City Transit System has successfully initiated the "adopt-a-station" program, funded jointly by DOT and the National Endowment for the Arts.

In New York's adopt-a-station program, the community surrounding a transit station in effect "adopts" that station and tells the transit agency what sorts of artistic, aesthetic and design elements they want in their transit station to reflect their community. New York is also developing a cultural subway project which would link some of the subway stations, through maps and graphics, with the above-ground cultural facilities so abundant in that city. There is already a "culture bus" to the main areas of cultural interest in Manhattan. With one ticket, passengers can take any bus and get on and off repeatedly during the day to view these various facilities.

The mass transit program has funded transit malls in Denver, Long Beach and Portland which include aesthetic amenities for pedestrians. It has also funded the efforts of the Massachusetts Bay Transit Authority, which operates the Boston area subway system, to include the arts community at a very early stage of planning a new extension to the subway system. This "Arts-on-the-Line" project is intended to assure that art is not an afterthought but an integral part of the new transit development.

Railroads will be a viable part of our national transportation system, at least in some areas of the country, for many years to come. Therefore, DOT is funding the Northeast Corridor Project, the improvement and renovation of rail passenger service from Washington, D.C., to New York and Boston. Three-quarters of one percent of the station renovation funds are being set aside for art works in stations in Baltimore, Philadelphia, Newark, Wilmington and the other cities along the corridor.

The Department of Transportation also has a major federal aid grant program for airports, including terminal construction and improvement. The Federal Aviation Administration has issued an order encouraging the early consideration of design concerns for airport facilities and making funds available for original works of art in air terminals. Atlanta was given a grant of $200,000 to incorporate art into the newly expanded Hartsfield Airport terminal. San Francisco Airport, Sea-Tac Airport in Tacoma, the Miami airport and others have also incorporated art work or in other ways paid particular attention to the aesthetic quality of their terminals. Dulles Airport terminal outside of Washington, D.C., is generally considered to be one of the great pieces of architecture in the United States. It is not only a beautiful structure, but it is extremely functional and a pleasure for the passenger.

However, the congressional Appropriations Committee wrote into the department's FY 1980 Appropriations Act that DOT airport grant funds were not intended to be and should not be used for the purchase of art work. We will continue to encourage the use of art in airports, but will not be able to provide funds directly for that purpose.

Regarding the second Department of Transportation initiative, improved procedures to integrate art and transportation, a Departmental Order was issued mandating the consideration of design and aesthetics in the very early stages of transportation planning, with discussion in environmental impact statements (E.I.S.) where relevant. Such environmental impact statements must be circulated to local and state arts councils for comment. If you have not been receiving these E.I.S.'s for comment, get in touch with your state or local transportation agencies.

Department of Transportation procedures for selecting architects and engineers are also being revised to assure that the design capability of the architects and engineers is a factor in their selection. Some grantee agencies have a very close relationship with a particular architect or engineer, and there presently may not be adequate consideration of what other architects and engineers have to offer in terms of design and aesthetic capabilities.

The third initiative concerns research, development, training, and information. DOT is currently developing, through an outside consultant, a series of guidelines on improved aesthetics in transportation. This document will compile examples of the best state of the art in aesthetics in transportation facilities. It will be fully illustrated with photographs of the best examples of aesthetic considerations and works of art in transportation facilities throughout the country.

A demonstration program with the New England Municipal Center is currently underway to assess the opportunities for small communities to use their transportation facilities to enhance the aesthetics of those communities.

The Federal Highway Administration (FHWA) has conducted a series of studies and is making information available on the results. One is a report on the visual quality of noise barrier designs. DOT has been trying for the past few years to mitigate the adverse impact of noise in transportation facilities, particularly on highways. One of the major techniques to accomplish this is the construction of noise barriers. Unfortunately, the earlier barriers were quite ugly, so a study was developed to see how those noise barriers could be made more aesthetically pleasing, both to the traveler and to the surrounding community.

The Federal Highway Administration is also conducting a study and will be publishing a report on the visual impact of proposed highway projects. Another study is planned on design and aesthetic considerations for highway bridges and grade separation structures, which can sometimes be quite attractive. A study is also being done on the design, location and evaluation of urban street furniture, and on tunnel design and its effect on motorist attitudes.

Another FHWA information project involves collecting photographs of highway art for use in promotional material on art in the highway program. FHWA is developing a brochure on good visual design of highways and roadside facilities, and they have funded a pedestrian mall exhibit as part of the New York City Cooper-Hewitt Museum's exhibit on urban open spaces. In addition, FHWA offers an excellent course on aesthetics and visual resource management for highways; if you think your state and local highway officials are not sufficiently sensitive to aesthetic considerations, urge them to attend.

The Urban Mass Transit Administration's "Arts-on-the-Line" project in the Boston area will develop a report for national circulation on how the arts community can effectively work with transit agencies. UMTA has also awarded a contract to produce guidelines for the aesthetics of advanced guidance transit systems, the

so-called downtown people-movers, which are
planned in a selected number of urban centers.
Installing such a facility above ground in a
dense, already existing urban core, and
fitting that facility in an unobtrusive and
aesthetically satisfactory way will be quite
a challenge; the UMTA guidelines project is
intended to provide assistance to urban areas
to meet this challenge.

The United States Coast Guard, part of the
Department of Transportation, is conducting
an inventory of their buildings to assess
the opportunities for historic preservation
and aesthetic enhancement. They have many historic lighthouses, for example, which are on
the National Register of Historic Places, and
they are looking at how these can be preserved
and utilized for the public.

The Federal Aviation Administration has developed
a slide show, which it is showing to airport
authorities around the country, entitled "A
First and Lasting Impression," on the use of
good design and aesthetics in aviation facilities.

Finally, DOT has established several awards
programs, one in the Federal Highway Administration, one in the Federal Rail Administration and
one in the Federal Aviation Administration,
to provide incentives for aesthetic design and
the use of art in transportation facilities.

The fourth initiative established by the 1977
transportation and the arts policy statement
concerned graphics improvement and transportation symbol signs. An internal graphics improvement program is already underway at the Department of Transportation. A contractor has made
recommendations for changes in our internal
signs, stationery forms, and graphics, and he
is developing a graphics standards manual for
use throughout the department. We have also
developed a set of fifty-two new transportation

symbols and signs which we hope will become the standard.

The Department of Transporation is attempting to accomplish the fifth initiative, monitoring the overall design quality effort, by use of a departmental design quality task force. The Office of Environment and Safety chairs that task force and provides staff support. DOT has also been working with other federal agencies, exchanging information through such means as the Federal Design Assembly and the Federal Council on the Arts and Humanities.

The Department of Transportation, through increasing its funding for design and arts, through improved procedures, through research, information and training, through new graphics design, and through monitoring the coordination effort, is attempting to utilize its more than $10 billion in transportation grants to help improve the aesthetic quality of transportation facilities and the environment in which they exist, and to encourage state and local transportation agencies to do the same.

The effort is serving as a prototype for other government agencies, and we expect shortly that all federal agencies will initiate similar agency-wide efforts to improve their contribution to aesthetic and cultural activities.

In conclusion, I would urge members of the arts community to make an effort to utilize the opportunities that our programs, policies and funding provide. Our funds go to state and local transportation agencies. If the arts community seeks out these agencies, encourages them and works with them to use our programs, an effective partnership can be achieved.

Together, we can help to make transportation facilities and systems a positive contribution to the aesthetic quality of the nation's built environment.

The Arts and Social Services

by Reynold A. Boezi
Director, Warren-Sherman Project,
City Venture Corporation

One of the difficulties for a planner trying
to work with the arts community is that art
means many things to many people. There is
nothing wrong with that, but there is something wrong with suggesting that art can be
narrowly defined. If there is anything about
which there is tremendous disagreement, it
is the series of questions: What is art?
What is good art? What is lasting art?

One dictionary definition of art is: an
expression of what is beautiful, appealing
or of more than ordinary significance. Another
is: self-expression, something aesthetic as
perceived by individual artists; creativity.

When one looks at those who "consume" art as
opposed to those who produce it, one sees
clearly that art is a matter of personal taste.
To some extent, good art seems to be what
critics say it is or what a consuming public
buys or what performances they attend. Great
art may be that which endures from one generation to another and finds its way to institutional settings: museums, galleries, theatres,
concert halls, etc. But the buildings that
house art are not necessarily art themselves,
unless they are architecturally significant.
One hears too little about the production of
art; it becomes too easy to lull ourselves
into thinking more about the buildings than
the art.

Traditionally the arts have received funding
from private sources while social services
have received funding from public sources.

However, as resources have become scarcer,
the competition has become fierce. As a result,
the arts and social services have sought funding in each other's traditional areas. For
instance, public tax resources are now available to the arts not only at the National Endowment for the Arts level, but increasingly from
state and local sources as well. Similarly,
the social services have been competing more
vigorously in the private sector for both
foundation and corporate contributions.

For the purpose of comparing the arts to social
services, I am going to divide the arts into
three categories: (1) Production of art by
individual artists; (2) Art in institutional
settings: from passive forms of books, paintings and sculptures in their respective museums
or libraries, to active forms of dance, drama
and music performed by established companies
or groups of artists; (3) Community arts: a
very loose category, comprising art forms
oriented to cultural or social causes associated
with groups or community settings.

This last category currently is probably one
of the more controversial areas of the arts.
It usually takes the form of small arts groups
and organizations. Its focus can be a neighborhood, an ethnic group, or a target group such
as the elderly or handicapped. Its essence
is a group of people who share common goals
or beliefs and who use art as one medium to
express their cultural position. They are
usually organizations of volunteers and artists
who wish to work in this context rather than
practice art solely as individual expression
or within a traditional institutional setting.
They can range from black or feminist theatre
groups to art or poetry classes geared to the
elderly or handicapped. There is a huge range
and mixture--with all degrees of quality. Their

purposes are close to those of the social
services, which may make them suspect by the
balance of the arts community.

A comparison of these categories of the arts
to social services can then be based upon
purpose, clients, process, evaluation and
primary financing.

Social services are based upon the need to
provide for the health, welfare, safety and
education of the general population. There
is an emphasis on special needs, and the clients
are also those who meet the qualifications of
eligibility.

The process begins with some kind of a rational
base, some kind of observable phenomenon,
and is carried out by a professional staff,
many of whom have been around for generations
and have developed their own language and
mystique. They really are good at writing
grant proposals, and at what follows after
having identified a problem or a goal.

The process can be based upon a problem--for
example, that people don't have enough to eat.
Or, it can be based upon a perceived goal--
for example, that the elderly should be well
fed or well housed, because they have served
society through a period of time. In other
words, the process can be either problem-
based or value-based. Goals then are end
results or conditions being sought. Objectives
are the methods by which the process can be
measured. When you can measure objectives,
you are in a good position to write grant
proposals. Policies are specific courses of
action that will be used to implement the
objectives and plans.

When you try to fit art into comprehensive planning, you are trying to fit art into the above model, and that is not easy to do.

Evaluation in the social services can take the form of a public review process, with final approval by public or private nonprofit boards in accordance with rules and regulations established by funding agencies. In the social services the funding agencies, particularly ones like the Department of Health and Social Services, have extraordinary rules and regulations, forms, evaluation follow-ups, audits, post-audits--something of which the arts have never dreamed. But that is what comes with public funding because there is a need to prove that you did the right thing. This is done by filling out many complicated forms to prove that the money has been well spent. There are, as well, many established periodic evaluations, either self-administered or by outside consultants. Many of them are worthless. They are time-consuming, and they do not prove much. Then there is the usage by clients, otherwise known as the "body count," which is the most obvious way. One can argue that nothing is happening to these bodies you run through, but if you can show more bodies one year than you did another, fantastic. So arts institutions have that problem too--having to run more people through. Then there are also such things as the unreconstituted count. For example, how many times did you run the same people through? They get clever after awhile. If you kept your records that way, it would tend to be complicated.

Primary financing for social services is through taxes and donations. There are a great many private, nonprofit organizations funded through the United Way or a similar group in individual committees. Fees or partial payments, based

on client ability to pay, income level and
other things such as sliding fee scales and
more complex financial arrangements also are
prevalent.

Individual arts are based on a need for self-
expression. Its clients are whoever wishes
to partake and can afford the cost. Its patrons
are usually individuals and institutions--that
is, people who purchase or attend the performances or the patrons who fund them. The process is intuitive. It expresses the production
of various arts ranging from performing to
visual to written forms. Its techniques can
be learned in educational institutions, but
inspiration cannot be implanted and art prod-
ucts can only be copied. Its primary financing
is through purchases, donations and grants
which are predominantly private, but are growing more public.

Institutional art is what most people think
they are talking about when they talk about
art. It is based on the need to sustain and
improve the quality of the art form being
sponsored by the museum, theatre, concert hall,
art gallery, etc., as well as the need to sustain the institution itself. The clients are
whoever walks through the door, or pays the
price of a ticket. The clients are also patrons,
because the patrons have something to say
about how institutions are run. They sometimes
make large contributions. They have some
influence over what happens inside the institu-
tions--in exchange for that money. They often
are on the board of directors or trustees. And
they are not only part of the process, but are
clients. One of the reasons that the institutions are very inward-looking is that, to a
great extent, those who are making the decisions
about the direction of the arts are also those
who are deciding whether it is good or not. It
is a very closed process.

The process involves professional staff separate from the artistic staff. The artistic
productions or purchases for that art form
and/or that artistic company are decided by
that professional staff with assurance from
the board of directors or trustees.

The planning is closest to the kind of planning
that is done in the comprehensive planning
model. Planning for both annual operations
and for longer range is geared to preserving
and enhancing the institution, its reputation
and its particular art form.

Evaluation is done by the critics, the purchasers and by the professional staff with
the assistance of the board. Occasionally there
is an outside evaluation, although it is
usually tied to institutional goals--for example,
whether to expand the facilities.

Even in the case of institutional art, the
arts seem to be terrified of anything called
research. They seem to be extraordinarily
unhappy with anything that would be considered
objective by the social sciences. One of the
current movements is for economic impact studies
for the arts. A number of these studies are
not going to be things that the arts community
is going to like--either because they will not
understand what they mean (they are very
theoretically based) or because they will not
be self-serving. One of the problems for the
arts, if they want to compete with the social
services, is that they are going to have to
learn to do some research and to take the
consequences of some of that research being
critical. There seems to be extraordinary
resistance to anything that is negative. There
is a tendency almost to run consultants out
of town when they do not serve the institutions
who have paid them. There is great resistance

to the kind of evaluation that might be critical,
particularly if it might in any way impinge
on funding.

Why? There is a good reason why. Most of the
arts organizations, whether institutional or
any other type, are on a financial banana peel
and anything that would appear negative, that
would damage their reputations, could, in fact,
cut their funding sources or slide them into
the red. The arts are the only field in which
you are considered to be making it on your own,
or making it as an institution, when you get
50 percent of what you need out of earned
revenue. What business can survive earning
only 50 percent of its revenue? Even the
strongest arts institutions are lucky to pull
down 50 percent of their revenues out of the
box office or by selling their books, etc.

Primary financing is through purchasers or
consumers, and the patrons. The patrons are
individuals, foundations, corporations and
the federal, state and local governments. In
the case of patrons, arts institutions are
considerably better able to compete for these
funds than are other areas of the arts. In
fact, companies and private foundations tend to
worry about what might happen to their money
if they give it to some offbeat arts organization.
They tend traditionally to give their money
to fine arts institutions, where they do not
have to worry so much about them doing something strange that will cause adverse publicity.
Of course, the professional staff is key here.
It is a different arrangement when there is a
professional staff rather than an artist working on his or her own or as a volunteer.

The community arts movement is based upon a
need to reflect cultural or social expression.
The clients are the community and ethnic,

minority or target groups--whoever wishes to
partake and can afford the cost. Clients are
usually substantially fewer than those of similar
art forms in institutions. That is partly
because these groups are housed in old, broken-
down churches, on the street, etc. But then
they do not have the high overhead. That is,
of course, until they are brought into expensive
facilities.

There are always wonderful, energetic efforts
to raise capital costs in the arts community.
Then when it comes time for operating costs,
foundations and private corporations say: "We
don't do that because that ties up our resources."
For organizations that cannot conceivably raise
half of the revenue from the box office, this
puts them in extraordinarily difficult positions.
The alternative is to be housed in broken-down
churches and old firehouses and so on, and that
may not be the worst possible thing.

Again, the arts are not the buildings in which
they are housed. It can be very dangerous for
community arts groups to continue to insist
that they must have monuments erected to them-
selves--even if they are going to put four or
five of them together. Moreover, the operating
planning done for arts organizations in general
is very poor, and there is a need to bring
economists into this field.

Planning for the community arts movement is
done somewhat intuitively. The artists (there
are few paid professional staff of any kind)
decide what best represents their cultural or
social objectives. Planning is also short
range and often motivated by the twin needs to
find the appropriate cultural expression while
fighting to survive financially. That combina-
tion is extraordinarily important. For those

who have received applications from community
arts groups and find them very difficult to
understand, it is essential to realize that
these groups often are doing *everything*. They
are keeping the building from falling down.
They are raising whatever funds they can. The
artists are often doing the original art work
themselves while trying to run the organization,
to survive and to write grant applications
which they have never seen anything like before.
These groups do not have the professionals
skilled at writing the particular nomenclature
that gets money. They are in a very poor
competitive position against the artists'
institutions.

Evaluation is mostly in the form of self-
evaluation--by peer groups or boards. Maybe
it is ultimately by a neighborhood group or by
the critics. But critics are not very important in the community arts movement. Many
do not really have any interest in it; they do
not think it is very good art. Some of the
prejudice is based up on concepts of what quality art is and what is worth their marginal time,
where they should spend it. In fact, there
are so few arts critics that it is difficult
to understand why more of them do not go insane
attending as many arts events as they do.

Primary financing is through the consumers
and the patrons. Foundations and corporations
require a group to show that it has been in
operation a certain number of years and that it
has a wide level of support; in other words,
that it is a solid institution. By the nature
of community arts--volatile, changing, reform-
ing--those requirements are difficult to meet.

Community arts groups in particular disdain
professional administrators because they are
so hard-pressed for money that they cannot

see spending it on those salaries. They say,
"Spend every dollar you can on arts, performance
of arts, production of arts, and stay away
from all those arts administrators because all
they do is drag you down." This point of
view shows a lack of understanding of what
arts administrators can do. But there are
some attempts underway, through various kinds
of funding mechanisms and organizations, to
provide shared administrative services for
community arts groups.

I would say that it will be only a year or
two before states giving out millions of dollars
annually will require an accounting of what
difference this money had made to the arts and
to the community in which the money is being
spent. But the arts--particularly the community arts movement--are woefully unprepared
to carry on the necessary evaluations. There
is an apparent and real danger that the money
will be substantially cut back when the big
budget crunches come. Even persons who are
very influential, who are also art patrons,
cannot go to the legislature every year. We
can do all the hyping of art we want, but it
will not work unless somehow we can show the
tangible benefits of the arts to the tax-paying
community.

The National Endowment for the Arts, by comparison to other sources, is going to become
peanuts. The big money will be at the state
and local levels, because the Arts Endowment
is going to have trouble raising huge amounts
of money at the federal level.

The social services have begun to compete
vigorously in the private sector and are already
taking dollars away from the arts. As the
competition becomes increasingly fierce, the

arts will have to adjust if they wish to compete
successfully. We can go on suggesting that
it's all right to keep on doing things the way
we have been doing them and that somehow we
can figure out a way to make these funding
sources believe that culture is wonderful and
exciting and that, therefore, they should
fund it. But that strategy is unlikely to work
over a period of time. Funding will shrink
marginally--and then shrink absolutely. There
are many who claim that the new patron of the
arts is the public sector--the government--and
that is a scary idea. When you work with
taxpayers' money, you are in a different league.
Legislators have a tendency to support the
arts for reasons such as economic development,
which is a very limited concept.

The social services, in contrast to the arts,
have skilled professionals to prepare proposals.
They advance projects that are credible, that
meet credible societal needs. Whether these
projects all succeed in meeting their objectives
is another story; many of them do not. But
the arts are going to have to find ways of
breathing that kind of life into their proposals.

On the other hand, individual artists need to
be extremely careful to avoid having their
artistic freedom curbed by accepting too much
federal funding of the type that is categorical
or is in any way tied to some kind of performance
standard. The only financing individual artists
should accept from the public or the private
sector is funds that have few strings attached--
either rewards for past excellence or incentives
to encourage excellence in the future. It is
enough for artists to tolerate the arbitrary
opinions and judgments of those making the
initial funding decision. If they give you
the money, they should not have anything more
to say about what you do with it, unless you

must guarantee a product. But it seems foolish
to say that an artist has to produce three
paintings or one play in exchange for funding.

Institutional art is usually well served by
fine organizations staffed with professionals
or members in good standing in the community.
These are status arts or performing arts companies with loyal followings--people who come
and pay regularly. The main problem they have
in competing more successfully with social
services is that their goals and planning are
often geared primarily to institutional survival.
The public rarely understands the goals of
these institutions or the particular version
of the art forms they are trying to advance.

A more public, participatory process might help
to improve public understanding, perhaps suggest
new directions that institutional art might
pursue in these changing times. This process
could lead to strengthening public understanding
and perhaps to some larger block grants, although
arts institutions are the ones that have gotten
most of the block grant money to date. Still,
the numbers have been incredibly small. The
Ford Foundation gave $5,000 to 42nd Street
Corporation--whereas they would have given a
six-figure grant to a study of that magnitude
in a comparable social service area.

The community arts movement represents a dynamic
trend in the expression and meaning of art in
this society. However, the strengths of this
movement--its volunteerism, its rapid change,
its dynamics--are also its weaknesses. There
are few of these organizations with professional
or volunteer staffs who have the time to plan
for the future since the struggle for survival
is an everyday problem. The ability of community arts organizations is thus impaired in

the grantsmanship business. They are usually
unable to write, or to promise delivery, on
complex grants--or even sometimes simple grants--
even if their ideas or projects are socially
worthy.

Perhaps we should have institutional shepherding.
For instance, social services and institutional
arts organizations are assisting the community
arts movements. Some arts institutions provide
technical assistance. Some social service
agencies occasionally provide funds for arts
programs for the elderly and handicapped and
those in neighborhood settings. There are
many arts people that think such special programs should not be funded out of arts money--
that they are not art. But the community groups
themselves greatly fear being taken over by
the institutions. Why? Because they believe
the institutions will take what is best about
the community arts movement, that they will
capture it for themselves, package it and
produce it in some slick kind of show in the
neighborhood, that it will be the end of the
community arts movement.

Another problem is that arts organizations do
not seem to work with each other very well. I
sat in a movie theatre--originally an opera
house--and heard five arts groups, who between
them had $1.83 in their pockets, question,
almost hostilely, the people who were offering
them a million-dollar facility. They were not
talking about how they were going to pay for
it. But the arts groups were suspicious that
someone was trying to steal their art. Social
service agencies do not say that they do not
want a free building when someone offers it to
them. They would have banded together and written
a forty-page work program by morning. We have
to find collective ways to do things.

I do not know how to measure quality. I am
considered a Philistine because I dare to
insinuate that in the community arts movement,
perhaps quality is not the major issue. I do
not really believe that. But what I do believe
is that the quality measure is different from
the way in which the quality of art traditionally has been measured.

I strongly support the community arts movement.
I think it is the lifeblood of the arts movement. But community arts groups are not able,
now, to compete with arts institutions or social
services for grants.

An example of one of the unanswered questions
for the arts is how to attract more low-income
minority residents from inner-city neighborhoods
to arts programs. For instance there are
excellent free programs on Saturday mornings
run by the Toledo Museum of Art. The museum
has received a foundation grant to study this
anticipated utilization problem. It is clear
how little we know about the relationship of
low-income, minority people and their needs to
express themselves through the arts. Thus, the
dilemma continues, as must the search for how
to appropriately wed social goals and aspirations with the expression of art.

Main Street Is Almost All Right

by Denise Scott Brown
Partner, Venturi, Rauch and Scott Brown

"Main Street is almost all right" is a quotation from *Complexity and Contradiction in Architecture*, a book by my partner, Robert Venturi. He was trying to suggest that in many urban areas, we do not need total demolition in order to start again, but rather, need to understand very well what a town is all about and help it to be better in the ways it wants to be. This has been my approach to a series of Main Street projects with which our firm has been involved.

Our first project of this type was undertaken in the late 1960s. South Street in Philadelphia was an old commercial strip threatened by extermination to make way for an expressway. A transportation plan proposed for the city claimed that the expressway would serve to separate the new redevelopment area to the north from "undesirable land usages" further south. The mainly black population that lived to the south rightly interpreted "undesirable land usages" as meaning them and, as the people who would be removed by the expressway had nowhere else to go, this created an angry, divisive situation in the city. It was only resolved when the community became convinced that there was no real need for the expressway.

"Advocacy Planning," a form of socially-based, grass-roots planning of which our South Street project is an example, evolved during the upheavals of the 1960s as part of the emergence of the

---

social planning movement in urban planning. We
learned several important lessons in social planning through this project. The first was that to
save a main street like South Street, it is necessary to find regional uses for its architecture,
but uses that will not displace poor people. We
discovered that South Street had an interesting
regional market, drawing people for a variety of
purposes from New Jersey and the outskirts of
Philadelphia as well as from the central city.

We learned that effective planning for inner access
to old cities involves regional economics, local
economics, historic preservation, knowledge of
architecture, knowledge of construction, and knowledge of local urban communities and of democratic
methods for achieving concensus.

Planners should be prepared to offer three services
to such a community: a careful interdisciplinary
analysis of its problems; the building of concensus
through a series of organized town meetings and
discussions; and high level design advice about
what to do in an old area that is ailing economically but that has a beautiful architectural
heritage.

A few years after the South Street project was completed, my firm was approached to make recommendations for The Strand in Galveston, Texas. Again,
this was a fine old commercial street, but it was
left high and dry because the harbor had been
moved further out to sea. Some warehouses were
still functioning in the area, but the beautiful
Art Deco railroad station was empty. There were
slight beginnings of new uses in the buildings,
boutique-type stores appealing to upper-middle-
class tastes.

Our analysis of The Strand area included land use
analysis, economic analysis, transportation analysis, and cultural analysis. As the success of The

Strand hinged upon finding new markets and over-
lapping regional markets, we set out the options
for activities that could make night and day use
of the available buildings--lunch hour activities,
tourist activities, etc. In 1964 there were a
great many vacancies on The Strand, but by the
early 1970s, when the study was commissioned, the
erection of two large office buildings nearby had
already initiated The Strand's rehabilitation.
This work has proceeded--warehouses have been reha
bilitated for apartments, offices, and stores--and
there is now commercial and cultural activity up
and down The Strand. Restaurants, boutiques and
antique stores abound and draw lunch-hour and
evening shoppers and tourists.

An understanding of urban linkages was important
to our understanding of The Strand. We made a
tentative activity mix study, that is, a study of
what kinds of activities people might combine on
one outing--a trip to the library on the way back
from a shopping trip, for example. Cultural resource planners in particular should understand
urban linkages in order to ensure support of cultural facilities.

We were also asked to suggest design guidelines fc
the rehabilitation of the buildings on The Strand.
We recommended retention of its characteristic
brick, but with the use of trim colors darker thar
the brick to help make the buildings appear mellov
rather than dilapidated. We also initiated a sigr
ing system for The Strand that included signs for
the causeway, banners and historical markers--a
system that is both attractive and evocative, that
is civic in its intention as well as functional.
The design guidelines and suggestions were intend(
to leave wide leeway for individual creativity.
They were not intended to constrain the sometimes
incongruous juxtapositions that are found in citi(
and that give them vitality.

While our work in Galveston continued, we were
preparing a Bicentennial exhibition for the Renwick
Gallery of the Smithsonian Institution in Washington, D.C. This exhibition, "Signs of Life, Symbols
in the American City," was in part an analysis of
symbolism in the traditional American street; not
the neon symbols that define the Las Vegas strip,
but symbols that form part of the buildings that
line the traditional street and communicate to
people through their symbolism. These might include a Renaissance-style office building or a
Greek-style bank.

Main Street itself is a symbol. Reproduced by
Disney for its symbolic value in Disneyland in
the heart of suburban Anaheim, it is available
in real life as a symbol of old-time values in
other suburban and rural hinterlands.

In 1977 our firm was hired as the planner for Old
City in Philadelphia. This is a wholesale and
warehouse district on the Delaware River north of
Society Hill. The oldest street in continuous
residential inhabitance in America, Elfreth's
Alley, is in this area, as is Christ Church;
Independence Park is adjacent. About ten million
visitors come to this general area each year. The
alleys that crisscross the area are currently the
main focus for residential use because they are
much quieter than the main streets.

Before urban renewal, artists had moved into the
loft buildings in this area, making it a sort of
Philadelphia Soho. Now, of course, the artists
cannot afford it anymore. The people working and
living in Old City are as diverse as the uses of
its buildings. To achieve methods for ensuring
democratic concensus in planning, the city appointed
a steering committee which represented various
interest groups: the merchants, wholesalers, artists, residents, citywide interests and, in this
case, a strong historical lobby. Regular meetings

were held, with the members of the committee reporting back to their constitutent groups. A
great deal of trust was thus formed among the
members of the steering committee as they worked
with each other to achieve a concensus within the
the community at large.

The small town of Jim Thorpe in the Poconos of
Pennsylvania has a picturesque Main Street that
winds up a valley between steep mountain slopes.
It was once one of the richest towns in the United
States because coal was discovered nearby, but tha
was over long ago. Today, Jim Thorpe survives on
a modicum of tourism and on the fact that it is a
county seat. Meanwhile the region itself is a bur
geoning recreation area for skiing and canoeing.

We recommended that Jim Thorpe use its heritage of
historic buildings, its fine old Main Street and
its river location to establish a unique regional
identity that would help it to attract recreation
visitors. However, we warned that these economic
forces should be tapped carefully if they were to
serve, rather than overrun, the citizens of Jim
Thorpe.

Essentially, we advised the town to reestablish
its historic connections between Main Street, the
rail, the canal, and the river. By achieving this
larger identity, we felt the town would not need
to "Victorianize" its already Victorian buildings.

We recommended retaining the mixture of primarily
Victorian buildings interspersed with some later
additions found on Main Street. Most of our recom
mendations were quite specific and for the short
run: use of an area that had been demolished; in-
sinuation, very carefully where it would not show,
of a parking structure; rehabilitation of the exis
ing buildings; and some parking space by the railroad stations.

This type of planning has a component of architectural analysis that is more detailed than architects are accustomed to performing, and it requires regional analysis that is broader than the analyses planners usually perform. It requires, too, an attention to democratic process that is time consuming and emotionally demanding. However this broadening of the scope of planning beyond its usual boundaries will result, we feel, in plans that will have a greater chance of implementation.

If one is interested in how cities get to be orderly and beautiful without too much direction from planners, one turns to analysis of such cities as Las Vegas and Miami Beach. In both of these unusual cities, there is a strong sense of unity amid the variety on city streets and one can hazard guesses at the determining forces that brought this about--sun, desert, gambling, the drivers' reaction time, and a parking ordinance, in Las Vegas, and sun, ocean, the island topography, the hotel business, and zoning in Miami Beach.

Miami Beach also has another order of architecture, much more modest. When in 1972 I first visited South Beach and saw its Art Deco buildings, I contacted the local chapter of the American Institute of Architects urging them to preserve the world resource that was right under their noses and not to demolish it before it had even been recognized. A few months ago, the Deco District was named the first historic architectural district less than fifty years old. Now, its future is assured by a cast of thousands, in Washington and locally.

In 1977 we were hired as planners for Washington Avenue, the main street of South Beach in Miami Beach. Although beautiful Art Deco buildings line the streets of South Beach, the main street itself is tawdry. It has a variety of stores of different heights and sizes, many of them underused, and it has the remains of a Hollywood-type Palm Beach landscape. The area is fascinating economically because people come from Latin America, Northern America and Europe for an inexpensive holiday, and old people, mainly Jewish, come from all over to find the sun. There are Cubans moving in as storekeepers and entrepreneurs. The result is kosher delis and Cuban restaurants. Many of the Cubans are Jewish. Medicare is an important part of the economy of this area. Old people have money, through food stamps and through Medicare, and this cannot be ignored in an analysis of the economy of such an area.

Our plans called mainly for small-scale improvements in the streetscape and landscape of the public sector of Washington Avenue. Shaded seating alcoves and well-meshed street crossings were particularly important for an elderly community. Our design guidelines for the rehabilitation of buildings along the avenue suggested pastel colors for the stuccoed store fronts, with striped awnings over store windows, and use of the stucco facias above the awnings for signs.

It is important in this planning to help the community find sources of funds for implementation. In the last ten years sources have fractionated and the sums have become smaller. We provide rather detailed implementation schedules, starting with year one and proceeding year by year. These list sources of funding from different local state and federal agencies. Communities must find funds for planning, too. The planning approach I have described, that tries to preserve beautiful old environments by increasing their economic viability without overwhelming their occupants, calls for careful nurturing, dedication, and particularly time, from the planner. If such project remain as they are now, primarily labors of love, few will be undertaken by planners in the future.

Funding: Sources and Processes

I. by Robert McNulty
President, Partners for Livable Places

The words "cultural planning" will not be found in any city planner's manual. They are not yet written into any legislation as such. Cultural planning is not a pure discipline, not a profession. It is a sort of half-breed among a number of areas that deal with arts and urban planning. Typically, mixed disciplines like this have great difficulty in getting funded. One way to overcome that difficulty is to look to some successfully funded planning programs initiated in the past that led to the establishment of this field.

The Department of Housing and Urban Development's 701 Conference of Planning Assistance Program, for example, provided funding for comprehensive planning which really led to the establishment of regional planning in America. That program still is alive; it has not had much political support lately, but it would not be beyond the imagination to see special language included the next time the Housing Act is reviewed that focused on 701 planning assistance for cultural planning in our communities. That would be an easy way to earmark a specific federal dollar for cultural planning and might lead to the establishment of the discipline of cultural planning.

Consider the example of the Historic Preservation Act of 1966. Before the Historic Preservation Act, there was no comprehensive inventory program for the development of historic resources in most states. After the passage of the act, the first assistance was given on a 70/30 match basis; that is, the federal government paid

70 percent of the costs, while the state was
responsible for 30 percent. To qualify, states
had to institute a planning process to take
into account their preservation resources,
and this planning process had to begin before
any capital grants were awarded. Thus, the
whole system of state historic preservation
officers, of state inventories, of the national
register was created from the inducement of the
70/30 match for beginning the planning process.

I think if we are serious about cultural planning, if we do wish to merge cultural, arts
and physical planning together, there will have
to be a federal subsidy and that subsidy can
come from a minor adjustment of existing legislation. But it will take political backing,
and it will take some interest from constituents
to express this to their congressmen and con-
gresswomen.

Perhaps the best place to secure resources for
cultural planning is the Design Arts Program
of the National Endowment for the Arts. The
Arts Endowment very successfully almost doubled
its budget last year and has $5.5 million slated
for this year. It should prove to be a valuable
source of funding for cultural planning.

Beyond the Arts Endowment program, however, I
think planners are probably left with what they
have been doing all along: catch as catch can.
These include a variety of federal resources
not really set aside for cultural planning, but
in fact available for that purpose. I am going
to touch upon a few you may have overlooked.

The National Endowment for the Arts, for example,
offers far more than the Design Arts Program,
including the Expansion Arts Program, the Federal-
State Partnership Program and Special Projects.

At the Department of Housing and Urban Development, there is the Community Development Block Grants program, the UDAG program, the 701 grant program and a technical assistance offering. All of these could be used in some form or another to advance a framework for merging the arts and physical planning.

At the Department of Commerce, if you live on a coast, there is the Office of Coastal Zone Management. It may be a resource, if you are talking about a waterfront city and the relationship of tourism to cultural and physical planning. The Economic Development Administration may also be a resource.

The Environmental Protection Agency has a special interest in trying to develop a larger constituency for mixed use and multiple use of sewer systems, land fills and infrastructure investments. If there is some way that that can be related to physical planning and in turn related to a quality of life and culture, I think EPA would be delighted to join a common cause.

The Department of the Interior has a five-year Urban Parks Program which sets aside 10 percent of its $400 million for innovative projects; innovative projects might very well be defined as cultural planning relating to parks and recreation within a city, particularly in a low-income area. This department also offers an extensive technical assistance program.

The Department of Transportation, within the Urban Mass Transit Administration, has a vested interest in cultural planning, especially as it relates to energy conservation, as cultural activities are normally within the central city. There are certain important implications to restricting cars and reducing commuting time, for example, and I think there are some innovative grants available from the Department of Transportation to explore such possibilities.

The Department of Labor's Comprehensive Employment and Training Act (CETA) is a resource that I am sure has been extensively used for planning purposes. The Department of Energy, because of its conservation interest, may be a suitable rider on some of your existing projects. And the Department of Health, Education and Welfare, in terms of its impact on culture, the family, education and community mental health, might be an additional source of planning dollars.

At this point I would like to cite several of the Partners for Livable Places' members and examine how they have targeted various resources from different perspectives. These are organizations that see culture broadly defined to include physical planning. One such member is the Municipal Arts Society of New York City, which views arts and culture from the point of view of public arts, that is, architecture, urban design, landscape architecture. Yet it is also involved in the performing arts. Thus, the Society has become a model for the city's urban groups and arts groups. But beyond that role, as a private citizen body, it also wrote the first zoning code in America, and convinced the Board of Estimate in New York to pass that code. It also wrote the Historic Landmarks Ordinance for the city. How many of your arts councils or civic bodies are taking the lead on such complex physical planning design issues for your city?

Take another perspective, the East Los Angeles community in Los Angeles. Here was a community virtually without arts, where the primary concern was employment. But that has turned around, and now the East Los Angeles Community Union is a chief patron of the arts and culture in this area. Again, this is an example of a community development corporation viewing culture not only as a unifying force and a substance to the soul, but also as a provider of bread and butter and jobs for people in the area.

The Greater Jamaica Development Corporation, another member of our group, has a community development purpose involving the arts and culture. Ten years ago it began trying to put in artists' housing, works of art in public places and celebrations in the midst of the city to let people know that this was not an abandoned area, that there was activity and the arts could enrich their lives.

The city of Baltimore is attempting to change its image by using the arts and physical planning changes. This is a city where things are happening, the most exciting city in America today in terms of the blend of physical design of the arts and culture.

The Cincinnati Institute, a small group formed out of an arts constituency, has, like the Municipal Arts Society, tackled some very complex zoning issues. They came up with funding from the Arts Endowment to rezone the entire city's topography, hillside and slope to preserve environmental quality. They were able to develop the concept in two years and to get it approved by the city council in six months; considering how complex the issue of a zoning plan to overlap existing zones, one can appreciate what a feat this was for an arts organization.

The Pittsburgh Historic Landmarks Foundation,
another member, has become a patron of popular arts in that city. When it became too
difficult to go to the same wealthy foundations
each year to ask them for the same necessary
subsidy, the Foundation became a for-profit
developer. It now has $120 million of develop-
ment underway in the city of Pittsburgh, with
all of the profits collapsing into subsidy of
low-income home ownership in the poorest black
neighborhood in the city. Now, that to me is
a civic art, involving cultural planning in
who will stay in the city to enjoy the culture.

Lastly there is the example of the Pennsylvania
Avenue Corporation, which is attempting to
renovate and animate Washington, D.C.'s historic Pennsylvania Avenue. The developers have
realized that the arts and culture are the
only means by which to attract people from the
Mall, a strip of open space lined with museums
that stretches from the Capitol to the Washington
Monument. A number of the Corporation's board
and staff members went to Europe to learn what
roles the municipal governments play in animation and arts. Meeting with the mayor of
Copenhagen, they were told that the city planning director had two people on a staff that
programmed more than 12,000 public events a
year! As a result of their studies, the board
opted to create a nonprofit corporation, with
a part of their rents going directly to that
corporation for the animation of Pennsylvania
Avenue, using the arts, culture and celebration
as a resource to ensure the success of this
major investment of our taxpayers' money.

Clearly, then, there are necessary and creative
linkages which can be made between the arts,
culture and physical planning.

II. by John Blaine
Executive Director,
Cultural Arts Council of Houston

The various federal programs that make funds
available to the arts can make one's head spin
a little bit. There are so many, and they are
so diverse, that the possibility of actually
making contact with all of them and filling
out all of the necessary forms does tend to
boggle one's mind. It is sometimes a deterrent
to those of us at the local level who are
attempting to see programs work.

The way to create funding in Houston is to ask
Earl Campbell and "Bum" Phillips to come to a
party and charge $1,000 a head. Then you get
your program started, and there's not a lot of
reporting to do. One of the things that impressed
me most about the city of Houston was the spirit
of the people toward the Houston Oilers after
they lost to the Pittsburgh Steelers last year
in the playoffs. Forty or fifty thousand
people came to the Kingdome and welcomed home
a team that had lost.

That same spirit can be seen each year at the
Houston Festival, where virtually hundreds of
thousands of people hungry for experience,
hungry for contact with each other and with the
arts, come to downtown Houston, sometimes on
very hot and humid days, to participate, to
see what's going on, to be a part of a celebration and an experience. This feeling that
Houstonians are developing toward their city,
this pride about living there, was last year
manifested in the passing of a tax that is
going to lead to better mass transit. This
year another bond issue passed, with virtually
no publicity, that makes a great deal of money
available for drainage problems and street
maintenance.

In Seattle, where I started my career in city
government and the arts, there was that same
sense of pride about the city. Fortunately that
pride translated itself into phenomenal local
support for the arts. Our program became a
model, I think, primarily because our monies
increased so quickly. We went from a $60,000
budget in 1972 to something close to $2 million
by 1978. The National Endowment for the Arts
was in a similar situation. The focus was on
increased dollars, making the annual budget go
up and up. The focus around the country was on
getting more general fund money for the arts
and on increasing the number of corporate dollars
raised in combined corporate campaigns. The
slogan for the arts community in the 1970s
was pure and simple: Get more money for the
arts.

Various methods were devised to accomplish that
goal. Percent-for-art programs were founded
that provided fairly large amounts of money for
the commission of works of art and for involving artists. The Comprehensive Employment and
Training Act (CETA) of 1974, that began providing funds in 1976, now gives more actual dollars
to artists and arts people than the Arts Endowment itself. Hotel-motel tax laws were accessed
in San Francisco that allotted a percentage of
that tax to provide support for local arts activities. Local endowments, special bond issues,
special taxes or a one-time-only tax were all
tapped as possible sources of more money for
arts projects and arts organizations.

But in the 1980s "Get more money for the arts"
is no longer the energizing slogan. The 1980s
will be a time to put to good use the increased
funds we now have available. It will be a time
to focus on cultural planning and the integration
of the arts into a viable financial, social and
economic structure within our living environment.

This is already happening throughout the country.
New York City's 42nd Street project, for
instance, will change an area of disrepair
and disrepute into a place that can draw people
to very high-quality entertainment and that is
economically viable. Some of the income, the
profits as it were, from that experiment will
pay the costs of subsidizing the legitimate
theatres that are an integral part of the project. That is exciting; that is wonderful;
that is to my mind an energizing thing.

Another example of successful arts integration
is the Watts Housing Development Corporation
headed by James Woods, who started the Studio
Watts Workshop in California back in the early
1960s. The Corporation is made up of the Studio
Watts Endowment Fund, the Solid Rock Baptist
Church and the Westminster Neighborhood Association. Two low-cost housing developments are
already serving some 300 residents, and another
200 rehabilitated units are being developed
under the Watts Housing Corporation.

Jim Woods recognized early that the arts could
only be viable in his community, and I think
in any community, if they were part and parcel
of that community and not separated from it.
He saw the people's needs in Watts were for
identity, for mobility, for jobs and for housing.
So Woods asked local artists to act as liaisons
between the people who live in Watts and the
designers, architects and bureaucrats who control and make the decisions about what is going
to happen there.

It was a very slow process, but Watts is a
different place today than ten or fifteen years
ago, and part of the success story is the Jim
Woods story. It proved invaluable to have
artists involved as liaisons between the HUD
people, who put a lot of money into that project,

and the residents themselves. Now those artists are living in that low-cost housing area
and are providing services for the people who
live with them. The identity that the people
feel about the place they're living in is so
strong that deterioration is not likely to set
into this low-cost housing project.

What most successful cultural planning projects
have in common is effective leadership. Certainly to make things happen we have to have a
consensus among the people who make decisions.
But consensus without leadership is only consensus. In Seattle, for example, a man named
Paul Schell gave leadership to the task of bringing the business community and the arts community together, creating a plan that made possible
general funding for the arts in the city. In
Houston the hotel-motel tax, which generated
over $1 million a year in direct support for
the arts in that city, would not have been
possible without the leadership of the head of
the Chamber of Commerce Cultural Committee,
Britt Davis.

I would like to tell you a bit about how the
hotel-motel tax came about. Texas has a state
law providing for the limited use of hotel-
motel taxes to promote tourism in the state, to
provide for payment of bonded indebtedness.
Before the legislation known as the Harris/Semos
bill was passed two years ago, the total amount
of the tax legally able to be collected was 6
percent. Now an additional 1 percent can be
collected, which, thanks to a companion piece of
legislation introduced by legislator Lance Laylor
can be used to support the arts, humanities and
historic preservation.

With the Harris/Semos bill and the Laylor bill,
Houston, like many other cities in Texas, was
able to increase the tax on hotels and motels

by 1 percent and to enter into a contract immediately with the Cultural Council of Houston.
That contract gives the Cultural Arts Council
all of that additional 1 percent--this year
$1,730,000. That money provides for arts projects
for the cultural institutions in the city and for
the special projects that relate to the humanities
or historic preservation. By contract, at least
20 percent of that money goes for performances
at Miller Theatre, a Parks Department facility,
but we are hoping to change that. As an outdoor parks facility, Miller Theatre should
really be provided for by the city of Houston
through general revenue funds.

With our new city council, we are hoping that
we can get this idea across and that the city
of Houston will take more responsibility for
the support of the arts than simply providing
the 1 percent from the hotel-motel tax. We are
also hopeful that within the next year Houston
will pass a percent-for-art law so that one
percent, more or less, of the capital improvement
program can be used to purchase works of art,
commission artists to do works and involve
artists in the design of new urban facilities.

It is the city of Sacramento, however, that
currently has the lead in my mind in works of
art in public places because Sacramento is the
only place where the leadership at the municipal
level has managed to see the potential for putting a hook into their contracts with private
developers, a clause that makes those developers
responsible for using a percentage of their
capital for works of art.

The results of having an effective percent-
for-art ordinance can be seen clearly in the
state of Washington. A project was begun there
three years ago, and even before pencil touched
paper, artists were commissioned to complete

a design team constructing a new substation.
The artists, architects and bureaucrats all
sat down together from the first; the artists
had to learn a new language, but so did the
architects and bureaucrats. They had made a
commitment to each other to see the project
through, and so they did learn to speak each
other's language. And the same thing that
happened in Watts happened in Seattle because
the artists became the liaison between the
general community and the designers.

The final result was a substation in the north
end of Seattle that is beautifully integrated
into the community, that is well liked, perhaps even loved, by the community. It could
not be more unlike an earlier substation that
won a national AIA award for its beauty and
design, but that sticks out like a "well
thumb" in the middle of a ghetto area of
Seattle. The new substation has won national
AIA awards too. But more importantly, it is
not vandalized because it is loved by its
community. The difference I think is totally
the result of an artist involvement.

Washington provides us with yet another example
of the effective use of artists in community
projects. Some seventy-odd abandoned gravel
pits in King County, Washington, were going to
have to be brought back to some environmental
standard. But instead of just grassing them
over or filling them in, the Public Works Department went to the King County Arts Commission
and asked for help in discovering artists who
did earthworks so that these artists could work
on the abandoned gravel pits and, in fact, turn
them into works of art. The project coinci-
dentally proved to be economically cost-effective
the Public Works Department was able to do the
work and pay the artists for less money than
they had originally set aside for bringing the

pits up to Environmental Protection Agency standards.

Finally, I want to discuss the integration that is so necessary for the arts to survive in our society. A perfect example of such healthy integration is the Houston Festival I referred to earlier. This is a joint project of the arts council and the convention and visitors council. The arts council provides $50,000 of its 1 percent of hotel-motel tax funds to pay the artists. The convention and visitors council provides $50,000 from a similar percent-of-tax fund for the international promotion of the Houston Festival, the result being that after just one year of this arrangement, we have tour groups coming from Japan, from Mexico, from Western Europe.

The integration is clearly there to provide a flourishing of both tourist development and the arts in Houston. The tourists are going to bring money back into Houston, through the shopping they do at the hotels and the motels, and this is a cycle that the arts can take advantage of. Artists are responsible for making this tourism happen and therefore deserve to be paid; it is a very important part of the process.

III. by Andrew F. Euston
Urban Design Officer, Environmental Planning Division, U.S. Department of Housing and Urban Development

Bringing the arts together with local government through the use of federal funds, local funds and other kinds of packaging is an act of creativity that is essential if the arts are to flourish in our culture. It is the task of cultural planners to accomplish that act, and increasingly they are exploring an interdisciplinary approach as the most creative method.

Very recently the Department of Housing and
Urban Development (HUD) started a program
called Urban Environmental Design. It is
based on the National Environmental Policy
Act, a law which mandates an interdisciplinary
approach to environmental design, including
the social and natural sciences. This approach--
bringing people together from economics, market
analysis, engineering, ecology, architecture,
planning and the arts, as well as developers,
investors, bankers, and people from communities--
is making changes that are important to our
cities and that give them hope.

What those concerned with urban environmental
design (UED) are talking about are the issues
of urban design and culture--the ambience and
the livability of a city. We are talking about
historic preservation like that in Charleston,
or glamorous and spectacular urban design
achievements like the I.D.S. Center and the
Skywalk in Minneapolis. We are talking about
rehabilitation in communities where people want
to conserve rather than to destroy, about fixing
up homes for people who already live in them
rather than allowing "gentrification" and other
socially disruptive kinds of displacement to
happen.

We are talking about self-help and citizen
participation, about techniques of communication
between the public and private sectors and
about new modes of communication to reach the
average citizen with news of importance about
their environment. We are concerned about
making things more specific to help local officials and local citizens accomplish urban goals.

And we are talking also about a new order of
insight and documentation about urban design
itself. This comes, for example, from the work
of a man whom I call the "Zen Master" of urban

design, Weiming Lu. This new order that is
emerging, which is indiginous to our arts, our
culture, our administration, we happen to call
urban environmental design. It is something
that is mandated not just by the changes in our
cities, but also by the pressures that have
forced those changes. Congress, in one step
after another, has enacted design related legislation to deal with the problems of cities--for
preservation, for accessibility, for relocation,
for energy, etc. Often these laws conflict with
each other, creating various programming and
funding pressures. The task of design administration is to integrate this whole host of issues--
including architectural barriers, preservation
and energy as things are built.

At HUD we have introduced a provision for Urban
Environmental Design to be an eligible administrative cost within the Community Development
Block Grant program. That means that a mayor
can determine which kinds of urban environmental
design activities will take place using HUD funds
from the city's block grant program. Thus, any
city can begin to reassess the way it uses
administrative funds and can bring more design
and cultural factors into play.

HUD's Community Development Block Grant program
provides approximately $400 million a year to be
divided among all the cities that want it. About
10 percent of that is set aside for administrative purposes, and it is this 10 percent that
can be tapped for what we are talking about here
as design process and the arts. Also, there are
programs like UDAG (Urban Development Action
Grants), with $400 million a year. For example,
the city of San Antonio used a UDAG grant to
finance a pedestrian link from the Alamo Plaza
to the River Walk. Then there are HUD's housing
programs--312 rehabilitation, Section 8 housing
and so on.

It is a myth, however, that there is 1 percent for art in all these HUD programs. There never has been such a massive source of support for the arts. There used to be a 1 percent for art optional provision in the urban renewal program, but that program has been replaced by block grants, an arrangement in which the arts must compete with every other expense. A 1 percent for art optional provision in the public housing program does still exist, but it has to be taken out of the hide of projects, and in public housing that can be devastating.

There are currently several HUD projects underway that seek to deal creatively with urban design and cultural planning. In one, twenty-two cities are working to share techniques among themselves to bring design quality into what is being built. It is called the Urban Environmental Design Administration project. Our contractor, the National League of Cities, is helping these cities demonstrate ways that city government can be modified to improve the decision-making process. City festivals, public open space, community facilities and private investment stimulation are some of the indirect ways cities are promoting the arts in this program.

There is also a research program going on with Rice University, Massachusetts Institute of Technology and the University of California at Berkeley to establish a tool kit, a cookbook for local governments, documenting successful ways to deal with the problem of integrating public and private investments with respect to the quality of the built environment.

A third effort is a publication due out soon called *City Sampler: Urban Design Administration Cases*, a Community Development program guide. Recently, to produce this document, HUD completed a series of surveys encompassing forty cities and 140 case studies. They include a wide variety of topics, such as what citizen groups can do or how city governments can reorganize small elements of their agencies, add new teams and reconstruct existing ones, in ways that have been successful around the country.

Codorus Creek, a large stream running through York, Pennsylvania that has been befouled by a paper plant upstream, is a case in point. The city of York had proposed a flood control project for the area following Hurrican Agnes, a project that would have taken nearly eighty acres of historic iron foundries, shops, homes and other buildings in the flood plain and demolished them. A number of people in the community decided that the unique architectural quality of this old community, one of the first capitals of the United States, rich in history and architectural integrity, ought to be preserved. Alternatives were introduced by citizens and today the community has an urban design strategy for bringing round-the-clock economic and social vitality to York's central core that includes boating, bikeways, shops and neighborhoods preserved for those who want to remain where they have lived.

These various technical assistance and research activities are based on actual experiences in local government design administration. When, in 1976, HUD added "Management Approaches" as a category of its design awards, many cities submitted entries with documented evidence that local government has been using design administratively to integrate and resolve the problem of fragmented decisions, fragmented agency activities, fragmented federal laws and so on.

Thus the process of urban environmental design that has evolved in some places is an increasingly

interdisciplinary one, drawing from the arts,
from federal and local governments, from the
design community, from professional and neighborhood people. Effective administration is at
the heart of the process, and two major issues
of administration are design control and design
review.

Examples of effective design control and review
include the city of Baltimore, which has a special
panel within the city government that looks for
potential cultural uses for buildings that
might otherwise be torn down. Baltimore's historic environmental legacy is being protected
by this kind of review. In the heart of Cincinnati's core, a new community center was built
which included a pool hall, a swimming pool,
a center for the elderly and a community service
center with a credit union, job consultation
activities, day care and so on. This facility
has used super graphics murals as an effective
visual connection with the main shopping street
of the community. Finally, the city of Trenton,
New Jersey, did what I think is one of the most
beautiful examples of open heart surgery on a
core area. Its Mill Hill Historic Park is within
a short walk of the capital, right in an area
of traffic, freeways and so on. The park is a
neighborhood refuge with a quiet river and soft
landscaped edges. Nearby there is a children's
playground and, adjoining it, a bridge that is
maintained as a pedestrian facility. There is
also an amphitheatre built right at the river's
edge.

In each of these three cities, Baltimore, Cincinnati and Trenton, the successes were largely due
to the use of design professionals as administrative officials within the bureaucracy. There is
no set formula for this, but it makes a significant difference when those in government have
colleagues at staff levels who can translate and
relate to issues of design and culture.

What follows, therefore, is a series of examples, taken from the 1976 HUD design awards, showing how the arts have been aided by local design administration. The first example is the Arts for Living Center, located in the Bronx, serving a community of black and Chicano neighborhoods that had once been Jewish and Italian. Here an old settlement house was expanded and designed to allow people to close off the street and have functions there--using the building as an amphitheatre. Within there are facilities of all kinds--practice rooms, recital rooms, performing space, dance salons, etc.

The Farmer's Market, in Lancaster, Pennsylvania, is an award-winning restoration of a classic nineteenth century farmer's market. The city's planners were recognized for their restraint in not changing the function of that facility nor the way in which people in that community have merchandised their produce for generations.

In Newburyport, Massachusetts, a series of buildings was to be torn down and a supermarket built in its place. Instead the city awakened and began a restoration process to preserve the old buildings, thereby creating a new heart for the city of Newburyport. Art festivals and celebrations now take place in the streets, which are strictly for pedestrians.

In Portland, Oregon, there is an award-winning square in the center of the downtown that serves the shopping area and office district lunch-hour crowds. Very cleverly sited over an underground parking facility, it is designed in such a way that people can fully enjoy themselves and relax, shielded from traffic and from noise.

The town of Hudson, New York won an award for creating the first facade easement ordinance

in the United States. Its main street was a
continuum of American architectural history,
including the only cast iron facade residence.
Facades that had been carved up and mangled
over time were beautifully restored. The
award was given for an ordinance, not for
design but for the legal instrument to implement design. This, of course, points to what
we are talking about here--the urban environmental design process, the decisions and tools
and incentives for getting what we want.

The city of Santa Cruz, California, I am told,
had never used federal funds for anything if
it could help it. Then, in the early seventies,
it began a comprehensive program of historic
preservation and conservation, replete with
revolving funds, a master plan, and an inventory
of what they had, as well as walking tours and
training programs for people whose homes were
being rehabilitated.

In Greensboro, North Carolina, the people in
the community of a new public housing project
were involved in decision making, choosing,
for example, the kinds of equipment facilities
they wanted for their children. Programs (for
management of the project's environs) were
worked out which were extremely important to the
upward mobility of the residents, programs to
help people to begin new careers and to find
jobs, using the needs of the project as a starting point.

An even more dramatic case, perhaps the least
distinguished architecture you can imagine for
a design award, is a loft building for the garment industry in Philadelphia. It represents
the work of fifteen different organizations:
labor unions, the state, local welfare agencies,
local development agencies--even people from the
arts. Because of this loft space, the garment

district of Philadelphia, which had been so
spread apart it was beginning to disintegrate,
was rejuvenated. People who would have lost
their jobs instead are assisted within the
building by day care, health care and other
social serivces activities. Upstairs they are
making wares, some of which are sold in shops
on the street level. The building itself has
become an expression of integration through
design administration.

I came from the city of New Haven, studying
architecture there at a time when most people
were unconcsious that the city was being torn
apart. The focus was on grantsmanship and the
gerrymandering of project areas to get funds
for urban renewal. The philosophy at that time
called for pumping lots of dollars into the
downtown. Neighborhoods weren't being considered,
nor were fine old buildings, and people didn't
yet view these as design problems.

In New Haven administrators were the people
who were making all the decisions about the
location of buildings, or about who would live
in them, how large they would be, the size of a
project's budget, etc. Only then, after all
those decisions were made, was a designer called
in. Rarely were the neighborhoods consulted.

Now this has changed. Today most city governments are employing their own style of urban
environmental design to bring about the evolu-
tion of cities in terms of integrating people's
concerns of and blending all the resources we
can bring to bear upon them. In the various
programs for HUD dollars, while there is no
stated mandate in HUD legislation that allows
for the arts or culture per se, there are ways
for urban environmental design administrators
to secure those dollars.

A National Perspective on the Cities and the Arts

by Louis Harris
Chairman, American Council for the Arts

In a time of national crisis, when this country is caught up in a test of our national honor abroad and in a draining period of double-digit inflation and an uncertain energy future at home, the nation's cities and the arts share a common lot. Both are struggling to find their identity in a time when national values and priorities are undergoing severe testing.

There are, however, some definitive facts about the cities and the arts which, taken together, might just give us those shreds of hope that we so desperately need in the days and years ahead, in the decisive decade of the 1980s. My facts are based on a monumental study my firm completed just this past year, a study for the Department of Housing and Urban Development of over 7,000 adults nationwide.

Let me begin by separating some fact from fiction about the cities. There is a prevailing wisdom among those who ordinarily speak or write about the cities that goes something like this: the cities are in real trouble; the net loss of population from the cities, if left unchecked, could leave them empty shells in the foreseeable future, with increasingly high numbers on welfare, an ever-larger minority population, and with shrinking tax bases. If allowed to take their natural course, America's cities could in time become ungovernable pockets of decay, a blight upon the nation.

Judging from the results of our survey, such a doomsday analysis of the cities could not be further from the facts. For example, when we laid it right on the line and asked people how society would be without cities--if they were wiped out in one fell swoop--only 11 percent nationwide thought the country would be better off. A clear majority of 55 percent felt America would be worse without cities--56 percent in the cities feel that way and 57 percent in the suburbs share that view, as do 55 percent of those in towns and rural areas.

Why do a majority of the people feel that the country would be poorer without cities? From a long list of indispensable elements in American life, we asked which were best--the cities, the suburbs, or towns and rural areas. On no less than ten key dimensions, the cities were in the lead: 39 percent said that the cities have the best public services, such as garbage collection, street maintenance, fire and police protection, followed by the suburbs at 33 percent. A plurality of 47 percent nationwide hold the view that the cities have the best parks and playgrounds, with the suburbs second at 32 percent. A majority of 62 percent feel that the cities have the best shopping facilities, followed by the suburbs at 28 percent. An even higher 67 percent believe the cities have the best colleges and universities, with the suburbs next but far behind at 13 percent. Significantly, 71 percent feel the cities have the best employment opportunities, followed by the suburbs at 13 percent, and undeniably the presence of job opportunities is a most critical ingredient in the quality of life. An even larger 73 percent single out the cities as having the best clinics, hospitals and health facilities, far more than the 16 percent who selected the suburbs. A massive 77 percent picked the cities as having the best selection of restaurants, far above the 14 percent who chose the suburbs. A still higher 78 percent said the cities have the best selection of movie theatres, much higher than the 12 percent who picked the suburbs. And 81 percent said the cities have the best public transportation, far outdistancing the suburbs at only 8 percent.

But the most important finding by far was that fully 90 percent of the people in this country believe the cities have the best and the most plays, concerts, museums, dance performances and other cultural opportunities. By contrast, a meager 4 percent selected the suburbs. Less than .5 percent picked small towns and rural areas, and 1 percent saw no difference in those opportunities What the people of this country are saying is that the cities of this nation are the indispensible home of the arts. They are *also* saying that the arts are inextricably bound to each other, and in this period of economic difficulty they will, as Benjamin Franklin once said, either hang together or each will hang separately.

It is one thing for people to claim that the city is superior in many ways. But in practice do they really make use of the city's purported facilities On nine key activities common to many people, the survey asked the public to recount in detail how many of each type of activity they engaged in duri the past year, and whether they did those activiti in the cities or elsewhere. The results are among the most startling in the more than 2,000 surveys we have conducted. Let me recount just what we found for that 40 percent of the population who live in the suburbs, for it is not news that sizable majorities of city dwellers engage in various activities in the cities.

When those who live in the suburbs want to go out and have a nice dinner, an even 50 percent of the time they go to the city and not to the suburbs to eat. When those in the suburbs attend a religious service, 44 percent of the time they make the trek to the city. Of all the occasions when suburban dwellers have to go to a doctor, a majority of times, 52 percent, they go not to a doctor in the

suburbs but instead in the city. When those who
live in the suburbs visit friends socially, fully
47 percent of the time they go to cities to see
them. On occasions when suburbanites buy furniture
or a major appliance, 46 percent of the time they
go to the nearest city. When suburban people go
to a movie, 53 percent of the time they go not to
a suburban movie house, but instead to the city.
Finally, at the top of the list, when suburban
residents go to an art museum, see a live play,
a dance or a concert, 57 percent of those trips
are into the city.

These facts say unequivocally that the cities today
are the social, shopping, health, spiritual and
cultural centers of life in this country. It is
not overstating the case to conclude from these
results that the much-maligned cities of America
turn out to be not simply indispensible, but the
pivot for those critical activities that people
need in order to live.

Does this mean that cities are seen as all sweet-
ness and light? The cities also bear a whole host
of crosses: 59 percent think the cities have the
highest divorce rate, 64 percent the worst housing,
58 percent the highest taxes, 63 percent the worst
public schools, 92 percent the most crime, and 83
percent the worst place to rear children. In fact,
of late, incidence of crime in the big cities,
comparatively speaking, has tapered off. The
sharpest rise in crime has been in the small towns
and cities in the southwest.

The most serious problem for the cities is the
child-rearing problem, with only 47 percent of
all city dwellers able to rate where they live as
positive for bringing up a family, compared with
78 percent in the rest of the country. The heart
of the child-rearing problem is found in what
people perceive as the decaying public school
systems in the cities. Parents see the public

schools as partners with them in rearing their
children, and without this support, feel compelled
to move out of their neighborhoods and their citie
Mark it well, public schools are a *sine qua non* in
overcoming the child-rearing stigma that cities no
bear. The height of irony, however, is that city
schools in so many cases, when faced with budget
crunches, turn to the arts as the first place for
cutting--the very same arts and cultural activitie
which are the strongest attractions that the citie
possess.

But the central finding of the study points not to
a long litany of hopeless problems for the cities
to solve, but instead demonstrates the key role
that cities play in the lives of the vast majority
of our citizens. Sadly, neither the cities nor
the arts are properly compensated for the critical
services they provide together.

Put bluntly, the cities and the arts have been
cast as mendicants, literally begging for support
from federal and state governments in order to be
saved from oblivion. Neither the cities nor the
arts need such poor handouts. Cities are unfairly
asked to fund themselves from an essentially residential tax base, while providing critical service
for the vast majority of city *and* noncity folks.
In turn, the arts are asked to derive support for
their respites of pure joy from the pittances of
admission prices and inadequate private sector
contributions. Both the cities and the arts are
being short-changed. Both the cities and the art
go largely unappreciated and unrewarded. The tax
system simply does not reflect the indispensible
contributions of both the cities and the arts in
making human life in the last fifth of the
twentieth century bearable.

If both the cities and the arts could, for once,
recognized as vital hubs of life in this country,
am positive that there would be a return of pride

and a quickened sense of community everywhere.
People could once again look forward to their
daily lives with more hope and resilience. This
potential to better the quality of the human experience is closer at hand than most in the seats
of power believe. Yet it will remain unfulfilled
if the charge that the cities are useless entities,
serving out their time until they finally self-
destruct, is not put to an end. So, too, the arts
will remain fallow, their growth stunted, their
creativity bottled up if they are viewed only as
a fringe indulgence, the last to be embraced, the
first to be put aside in an ordering of national
priorities. The people themselves are more aware
than our leaders in this regard. And sooner, not
later, they are going to strike out for these
precious resources.

As Archibald MacLeish said forty years ago, when
I was very young, "America is promises. But only
if the promises are taken. Take them now, not
later. Take them now, before it is too late."

Synopsis

by Wolf Von Eckardt
Architecture Critic, The Washington Post

There is a new mood in this country. It is a sober mood. But it is also a mood that strives no longer for material riches and an ever higher standard of living, but for cultural values and a higher quality of life.

This may have more to do with Vietnam than people realize. Until we were stopped in the Mekong Delta, we could, with impunity, abuse our environment and go west when it got too bad. Now, consciously or subconsciously, we know we have reache the final frontier. We know we must settle down.

Although statistically, the central cities may still be losing population, emotionally we are no longer running away from them. In fact, young professionals, who are our taste makers and life-style setters, seem to be returning to the cities. They are restoring not only old houses, but also the discredited old ideas and ideals of civilized city living, historic continuity, and culture.

This generation of middle-class, middle-income people in their thirties is different from its parents. It is somewhat better educated. It is making considerably more money because its women have joined the labor force in unprecedented number. It is less interested in having children.

This means that Americans now in their thirties are no longer interested in good schools and safe backyards, which is what lured their parents to the suburbs. Rather than spend their time and money on commuting, they tend to spend it on travel and culture.

Yes, the restoration of deteriorated houses in the
slums by white middle-income people sometimes means
that low-income people are displaced. But rather
than bemoan this so-called "gentrification," we
should deal with it constructively. The city
is always changing and churning. The re-popu-
lation and recovery of the center city benefits
everyone. Conversely, slums hurt everyone.
The poor cannot rehabilitate their slum houses
because they lack money. They lack money because
there are no jobs for them in the slums or, for
that matter, in the center city. Helping them
to jobs, therefore, seems to make more sense
than expecting them to stay in houses they cannot afford to repair in an environment that does
not encourage higher aspirations.

The challenge of urban America, and the imperative
of the energy shortage, is to put people and jobs
together. We must make our communities more
compact. We must provide decent, safe, sanitary
and affordable housing for low-income people
where there are jobs. Blue collar jobs have
moved or are moving to what is still called
suburbia but has turned into "spread city"--
ugly disurbanization. Every human endeavor
but farming--everything from apothecaries to
zoos--which used to be together in compact city
centers, and therefore easily and equally accessible for everyone, is now sprawled over the
landscape. As Louis Harris has documented, people
are not as enchanted with this disurbanized way
of life as we have been made to believe. The
old suburbs are beginning to lose population.

What seems about to happen is a big population
switch: White collar people are moving back downtown where the managerial, cultural, research,
communication and educational centers are located.
Blue collar and semi-skilled workers are moving
out to the urban fringe where their job opportunities have, for the most part, already pre-
ceded them.

This big switch will bring hardships for people
as well as for the environment. But it also
offers marvelous opportunities. To ameliorate
the hardships and capitalize on the opportunities, urban planning must become more intelligent, more comprehensive, and far more
effective than it is now. We must learn to
plan not just housing but neighborhoods; not
just transportation but equal and easy access
to the necessities and joys of life; not just
to zone "incompatible" people and activities,
but to integrate our society. Our goal must
be to plan and build for what August Heckscher
has called "the public happiness."

Only public happiness--an uplifting and inspiring
human environment--can, in the end, overcome
private unhappiness, of which there seems to
be far too much in this rich and blessed country.
I don't mean justified grief or the miseries of
poverty and illness. I mean the vague, self-
pitying unhappiness that leads to divorce,
psychotherapy, psychics, and pseudo-religious
cults--the unhappiness that usually results
from an overzealous pursuit of strictly private
happiness. This pursuit has led to the much
deplored me-me-me malaise, the ego trips and
selfishly escapist and indulgent disco-culture--
alcoholism, drugs, promiscuity, and much too
much loneliness.

Americans, as I said, now seem ready to plan
more creatively for a more creative life. And
that, I suggest, is what is meant by cultural
planning.

Public planning for the public happiness is
nothing new. It is no luxury. It is not
particularly difficult or complicated. It
can and must be made part of the public
interest in livable as well as viable communities. It is often closely allied with

historic preservation. Its benefits to the
human spirit are, of course, immeasurable.
Its benefits to the city treasury, however,
can often be counted in dollars and cents.
Intelligent planning of culture into community
development can attract investments to build
better communities.

It is true that cities were founded and extended
for a variety of reasons. They were built as
slave camps for Assyrian and Babylonian
emperors, as ceremonial meeting places and
shrines, as refuges and citadels, as centers
of government power, as trading posts, as
manufacturing centers and combinations of any
of these. But usually the city, as Mumford
put it "magnificently overrode the original
aims that brought it into existence." Aristotle
has said of this transition from base motives
to inspired human purposes, "Men come together
in the city to live; they remain there to live
the good life."

From Athens and Rome, via Florence and Paris,
to the Columbian Exposition of 1893 in Chicago
and "The City Beautiful" movement, the job of
changing the city into a generator of the good
life was assigned to selected artists and
architects. The final authority on what was
a good city, good art, and the good life, was
the artists' employer--the bosses in the palace,
the temple, city hall or other powerhouses.

This changed somewhat under Franklin D. Roosevelt's
New Deal. The idea of the Works Progress Administration, better known as WPA, was to provide
jobs for artists rather than glory for the boss.
This meant that the initiative for what was to
be done passed from the client to the artist.
The authorities did not dream up the Riverwalk
in San Antonio. In fact, they intended to

turn the Rio Grande into an underground sewer.
The idea there started with the people--people
like architect-artist O'Neill Ford.

Culture rising up from below, not passed down
from above, is also an important characteristic
of the new cultural planning impetus, the new
movement for community enrichment. This assures
popularity, pluralism, and whatever the
antonym for "elitist" is.

Franklin Roosevelt's WPA was not considered
a frill (except perhaps by those who hated
everything FDR did). In the depth of the
Great Depression, most people, including most
politicians, knew that, just as some of us
whistle as we walk through dark woods, we
need music, dance, theatre, painting, sculpture,
art and joy to give us courage in times of
stress and budget cuts. We need artistic enrichment even more when we are poor than in times
of affluence. In 1970, when the Boeing Corporation had to lay off 50,000 workers and there
was a severe depression in Seattle, Mayor Wes
Uhlman stepped up the city's art program by
half a million dollars. "We all must begin to
view the arts...as a basic city service like
police, fire protection, garbage collection, or
street paving...if we are to survive with our
humanism intact," Uhlman said.

Uhlman's statement suggests one way to assure
effective cultural planning: The creation of a
municipal arts or culture department alongside
the police, fire, sanitation, and highway
departments. More important than organizational
structure, perhaps, is the creation of a strong
partnership between the arts community and city
or county government, particularly its planning
department. But a good, strong partnership
needs good, strong partners. The arts must be
well organized. Different arts groups with

different interests and outlooks must nevertheless
be united and speak with one voice. Their
representatives must be truly representative.

It may or may not be a great, artistic idea to
paint the Washington Memorial in Day-Glo candy
colors. But the people of Washington, to say
nothing of the myriad committees and commissions
that would have to vote on this idea, would
hardly approve. Stuffed shirts that they are,
they may not find this glowing idea to be in the
public interest. And they might be right.

In other words, those who would plan our culture
for us should not be content with glowing ideas.
They must be sure, very sure, that their proposals are of general public interest and benefit to the community. That takes more than
artistic enthusiasm, or even what seems to you
and all your friends evident artistic merit.
It takes research into all aspects of the project,
precise analysis and accounting, and accurate
documentation.

Suddenly, America's past has a future. For
many reasons we are seized by a wave of nos-
talgia and an urge to contemplate our roots
and preserve our old buildings and townscapes.
"Progress" is put in quotation marks. We all
know how much historic building preservation
has helped the arts. Old movie palaces have
been adapted for use as concert halls. Railroad stations have been turned into arts and
crafts centers. Old loft buildings serve as
artists' studios. Fire stations have become
community workshops.

Thousands of lovely and lovable old buildings,
however, are still under the wrecking ball.
The quotation marks have not stopped progress
of the bulldozing kind. The continued momentum
and success of the preservation movement depends

upon continued good ideas on how to bring old
buildings and places to new life. It depends
upon continued inspiration and hard work by
artists, architects, conservationists and other
concerned citizens.

Good cultural planning, like good city planning,
must be good economic planning. We know that
cultural activity--be it a street arts festival
or a Lincoln Center--can bring life and bustle
to its surroundings. We have seen in many cities
that the arts can stimulate business and create
jobs--they can fill cafes and restaurants, attract
new stores and perhaps even tourists and tourist
hotels. But we cannot always count on it. We
must be sure.

Effective cultural planning, in short, involves
all the arts--the art of architecture, the art
of urban design, the art of winning community
support, the art of transportation planning,
and the art of mastering the dynamics of
economic development.

It is no job for dilettantes.

About ACA

The mission of the American Council for the Arts (ACA) is to promote and strengthen the nation's cultural activities. For the past twenty years, ACA has done so by providing national leadership in innovative programs and services that have a substantial impact on all the arts, all across the country.

Through its programs, ACA takes the initiative in developing new possibilities for arts involvement, working on key policy issues, and expanding the resources available to the arts. Through its services, ACA responds to requests from the field and strengthens local arts organizations by improving arts management skills and information.

Corporate contributors to ACA at the time of publication:

> Aetna Life & Casualty Foundation
> American Telephone & Telegraph Company
> Atlantic Richfield Company
> Bank of America
> Bechtel Foundation
> Boise Cascade Corporation
> The Bristol-Myers Fund
> Campbell Soup Fund
> Carter Hawley Hale Stores, Inc.
> Celenese Corporation
> Chase Manhattan Bank
> Chevron USA, Inc.
> The Coca-Cola Company
> Colgate-Palmolive Company
> Conoco, Inc.
> The Continental Group Foundation, Inc.
> Estee Lauder Companies

Exxon Corporation
Federated Department Stores, Inc.
Ford Motor Company
Gannett Newspaper Foundation, Inc.
General Mills Foundation
Getty Oil Company Foundation
Glenn, Bozell & Jacobs, Inc.
Gulf & Western Foundation
Louis Harris & Associates
Hercules, Inc.
Heublein Foundation, Inc.
International Paper Company Foundation
IBM Corporation
Lydall, Inc.
Metropolitan Life Foundation
Mobil Foundation, Inc.
Monsanto Fund
Mostek Corporation
National Westminster Bank, Ltd.
J.C. Penney Company, Inc.
Philip Morris, Inc.
The Proctor & Gamble Company
Prudential Insurance Company Foundation
RCA Corporation
Rockefeller Center, Inc.
Ruder & Finn, Inc.
Sakowitz, Inc.
Scurlock Foundation
Sears, Roebuck & Company
Shell Companies Foundation
Times-Mirror Company
Tosco Corporation
Travelers Insurance Companies
Triangle Pacific Corporation
Union Pacific Foundation
United California Bank
United States Steel Foundation, Inc.
Walt Disney Foundation
Western Electric Fund
Westinghouse Electric Fund
Wheelabrator Foundation, Inc.
Xerox Corporation